RAMBAM

Moreh Nevuchim
Maimonides' Guide for the Perplexed

PART I
CHAPTERS 1–49

Translated and Annotated by
Avraham Yaakov Finkel

YESHIVATH BETH MOSHE
SCRANTON, PA.

TRANSLATOR'S PREFACE

Undoubtedly, one of the most celebrated works on Jewish philosophy of all time is *Moreh Nevuchim,* Guide for the Perplexed, written by Rabbi Moshe ben Maimon, better known as the Rambam or Maimonides. The mere mention of the title evokes a sense of awe and the apprehension that "this is over my head." Presented in this volume is the first section of Part One which deals with why and how the Torah uses physical terms when describing Hashem. It explains many difficult passages in the Torah and the Torah viewpoint of man's intellectual capacity. The Rambam does away with the erroneous idea that God is corporeal. He makes it clear that such Scriptural terms as the "eyes" or "hand" of Hashem are used figuratively, and explains their true definitions. He shows why the senses of hearing, sight and smell are attributed to Hashem, but not those of taste and touch. He explains that the Prophets speak in metaphors and allegories, and why. He further deals with the limits of man's intellect and discusses the study of metaphysics.

Spanning the centuries, the Rambam's works are as relevant to us today as they were to the Jews of his time, eight centuries ago. His immortal words lift the veil of uncertainty, dissolve many of our qualms and misgivings, and, above all, strengthen our belief in Hashem and His Torah.

It is my hope that this translation will make the Rambam's lofty thoughts easy to understand and inspire the reader with the Rambam's greatness.

AVRAHAM YAAKOV FINKEL
Shevat 5757/1997

NOTE TO THE READER

The Rambam in the Chapters included in this book deals with the reasons why the Scriptures speak of Hashem in corporeal terms. He also explains how these terms are to be understood. For reasons touched on in his introduction, the explanation of these terms and the principles behind them were not arranged in methodical order. Some may find it helpful to read the chapters dealing with the fundamental principles first. To make it easier on the reader those chapters dealing with the underlying principles are listed in the Table of Contents in bold.

CONTENTS

INTRODUCTION

THE LETTER THE RAMBAM WROTE
TO HIS STUDENT, RABBI YOSEF
BEN RABBI YEHUDAH AKNIN.

Ever since you came to me from a distant country want-
ing to study under me I admired your thirst for knowledge and your desire for abstract theoretical knowledge
which you expressed in your poems. I thought highly of you
the moment I received your writings and lyric verses from
Alexandria, before I had the opportunity to test your intelligence. Still I thought, perhaps your ambition is greater than
your mental capacity. When you studied astronomy under me
after completing all the required preliminary courses, I was
pleased with your keen mind and your quick grasp. As I noticed your fondness for mathematics I let you tackle that subject, because it is a forerunner of metaphysics[1] which is the
ultimate aim of all knowledge. After I taught you a course in
logic, my high hopes for you were confirmed. I thought you
qualified to be taught the esoteric ideas contained in the
books of the Prophets, and that you would understand and
view them from the proper perspective. When I began to
hint at certain concepts, I noticed you wanted more detailed
explanations urging me to clarify some metaphysical problems. You asked me to teach you the ideology of the

---

[1.] Metaphysics is the branch of philosophy that investigates the principles of reality.
It asks: What is meant by existence or being. What is it to *be*? It delves into the
Oneness of God, His attributes, His incorporeality, the creation of something out
of nothingness, the human soul, angels, and many related issues. It tries to understand, among other things, how God Who is a purely spiritual Being created a physical, tangible universe.

1

Mutikallimon[2] and to tell you whether their arguments held water, or not. I noticed you picked up knowledge about these matters from other people, and you were perplexed, confused, and groping for the truth. I tried to hold you back from exploring metaphysics and urged you to continue your studies in a systematic fashion. My intention was that you find the truth in a logical sequence, and not approach it haphazardly. While you were studying under my guidance, I never refused to explain a difficult Biblical verse or a puzzling statement by the Rabbis. But it was Hashem's will that we part company, and you went your way.

Afterwards, as I recalled our discussions, I reached a decision that had been dormant in my mind for a long time. Your absence prompted me to write this book for you and people like you, no matter how few they are. I divided the book into chapters, as soon as I finish a chapter I will send it to you. Peace and best regards.

A "GUIDE FOR THE PERPLEXED"

My primary purpose in writing this book is to explain certain words that occur in the books of the Prophets. Some of these are words that have more than one meaning, and because of that, ignorant people understand them in the wrong sense. Then there are words that are used in a figurative sense, and ignorant people take them literally. There are also words with combined meanings; sometimes they are meant in their literal sense, and other times, figuratively. I do not intend to explain all these expressions to the broad masses, beginners, or

---

2. The *Mutikallimon* was a sect of Arab philosophers who tried to harmonize Moslem theology with Aristotelian philosophy. *Kalam* is Arabic for *"word,"* and *Mutikallimon* means "sages of the word." In *Moreh Nevuchim* (Part 1, chapters 71-76), the Rambam vehemently opposes their views and methods.

to people who study only the legal aspects of the Torah, [who do not need this book, since the study of the Torah includes all there is to know about God, His Unity, His incorporeality, and the mysteries of Creation (Shem Tov)]; for the entire purpose of this work is to teach the philosophical underpinnings of the true wisdom of the Torah.

The aim of this work is to enlighten a religious Jew who has been trained to believe in the truth of our Torah, who faithfully observes the mitzvos and the principles of ethics and morality, and studied the works of the philosophers and understands them; a person seeking the absolute truth, but finds it difficult to accept the literal interpretation of the Torah, because of the way he himself misconstrued certain words or heard their explanation from others. He is perplexed and baffled. [It seems to him] that, if he sticks to the rules of logic and renounces [what he thinks to be] the [irrational] meaning of those words, he is denying the fundamental principles of the Torah. And, if he accepts the simple meaning of these words, against his common sense, he feels he damaged his true belief. He is constantly plagued by these thoughts which give rise to fear and anxiety, pangs of conscience and a wrenching sense of bewilderment.

This work has a second aim. It tries to explain certain obscure allegories in the books of the Prophets that are not clearly identified as allegories. Ignorant and foolish people take them in a literal sense and find them absurd. Even knowledgeable people will be confused if they understand these passages in their literal meaning. But as soon as we explain the metaphor or merely point out that the passage is a parable, their doubts are cleared up. For this reason I called this book *Guide for the Perplexed.*

Metaphysics Only for the God-fearing

I do not think this work will clear up every doubt in the mind of those who understand it, but I do say it will settle most of the misgivings people have. No sensible person will expect me to deal with all aspects of any subject I introduce, or to review all the various meanings of a metaphor I expound. No teacher could do that, even if he explained it in person, let alone an author who writes a book. Some general principles concerning this point have been fully discussed in our commentary on the Mishnah. We mentioned that the expression Ma'aseh Bereishis, *The Story of Creation* means natural science, and that Ma'aseh Merkavah, *The Works of The Divine Chariot* refers to metaphysics. We explained the intent of the statement by the Sages, "The Works of The Divine Chariot may not be expounded even in the presence of one student, unless he is wise and able to think for himself, [for such a student will not have to ask his teacher questions, for these mysteries may not be explained explicitly,] and even then you should only familiarize him with the headings of the chapters" *(Chagigah 11b,13a)*. Therefore, you should not expect from me more than brief outlines. And even these outlines have not been arranged methodically in an orderly fashion, but are scattered and distributed among other topics. I did this so that, on the one hand, the truths [of metaphysics] should be visible, and on the other hand, they should be concealed [by being scattered, so the student cannot study this subject systematically.] Thereby not going against the Will of God, Who has decreed that the truths pertaining to His Essence should not be taught to the public at large, as it says, *"The secret of Hashem is for those who fear Him"* (Tehillim 25:14).

LEVELS OF PROPHETIC VISION

You should realize that in natural science, too, there are subjects that should not be fully explained, for example, the coming into being of primeval matter. Our Sages put is this way, *"The Story of Creation* may not be expounded in the presence of two."* If a writer were to explain these things in writing, it would be the same as expounding them to thousands of people. That's why the Prophets speak of these things in allegories, and our Sages, emulating the Scriptures, speak of them in metaphors and similes. There is a close relationship between the subject [of Creation] and metaphysics; and Creation is indeed one of the mysteries metaphysics looks at. Do not think that these profound mysteries can be thoroughly understood by anyone. Sometimes we have a flash of insight making the truth clear as day to us. But soon after our nature and habitual thinking patterns obscure the truth, and we return to a darkness almost as dense as before. We are like people who, although they see bright flashes of lightning, are still surrounded by the pitch-darkness of night. Some experience the lightning flashes in rapid succession, they seem to be in continuous light, and their night is as clear as day. This was the level of prophetic vision attained by Moshe, the greatest of prophets, to whom Hashem said, *"You must remain here with Me" (Devarim 5:28)*, indicating that Moshe would henceforth always remain on the level of prophecy (See Chapter 13), and of whom it says, *"the skin of his face had become luminous" (Shemos 34:29)*. Some see the flashes at long intervals; this is the level of most prophets. Others see a flash only once during the whole night. This is the level of those about whom it says, *"They gained the gift of prophecy but did not keep it" (Bamidbar 11:25)*. There are some to whom the flashes of lightning appear at varying intervals; others don't see lightning flashes, but a clear luminescent substance or some kind of iridescent stone that lights up during the night; and to them even this small amount of light is not steady, but shines off and on, as if it were *"the revolving sword blade"* (Bereishis 3:24).

These various levels apply also to levels of perfection in man. People who never saw light even for one day, but walk in continual darkness, are described as, *"They neither know nor understand; they go about in darkness"* (Tehillim 82:5). Truth may be as plain as the nose on their face, yet they don't recognize it. Iyov had them in mind when he said, *"Now, then, men cannot see the sun though it is bright in the skies"* (Iyov 37:21). They are the masses of ordinary people; there is no need to mention them in this book.

WHY THE TORAH USES METAPHORS AND SIMILES

You must understand, if a person who reached a certain level of perfection wants to share with others some of the things he learned of these subjects—whether in writing or orally—he cannot possibly explain them in a step-by-step fashion, as he could if teaching a science for which there exists guidelines and a methodology. When trying to teach others, he will run into the same obstacles encountered when researching the subject on his own. One moment everything seems crystal clear, and suddenly, the solution fades away. Flashes of insight appear, and at once they vanish, whether you study yourself or teach a large audience. That is why, great rabbis teaching metaphysics always used metaphors and allegories. When they were unable to find a simile that perfectly matched the idea to be illustrated, they divided the subject into different parts.

If we were to teach these subjects without the use of allegories and metaphors, we would be forced to resort to expressions so profound and other-worldly they would be just as incomprehensible as allegories and metaphors.

You know, that Hashem wants to bring us to a state of perfection and improve the well-being of our society. To that end He revealed to us the practical laws of the Torah. However, these laws can be fulfilled only if we have the proper mindset. To begin with, we must form a conception of the Existence of God, according to our ability. We can attain this only through a knowledge of metaphysics. But you cannot understand metaphysics unless you know physics, since it is closely linked to metaphysics. That is the reason why the holy Torah starts with the story of Creation, in other words, with physical science. Now, on the one hand, the subject of Creation is very important, but on the other hand, our ability to understand these concepts is very limited. In view of that, Hashem described these profound concepts which His Divine Wisdom found necessary to impart to us, using allegories, metaphors, and imagery. Our Sages put it succinctly, "It is impossible to communicate to man the stupendous immensity of the Creation of the universe. Therefore, the Torah simply says, *'In the beginning God created heaven and earth'"* (Bereishis 1:1). Thus they pointed out that this subject is a deep mystery, as Shlomoh said, *"[The secret] of what happened is elusive and deep, deep down; who can discover it?"* (Koheles 7:24). It has been outlined in metaphors so that the masses can understand it according to their mental capacity, while the educated take it in a different sense.

In our Commentary on the Mishnah we stated that we intended to explain difficult problems in the Book on Prophecy and in the Book of Harmony. In the Book of Harmony we planned to examine all the passages in the Midrash which, if taken literally, appear to be untrue and irrational, and must therefore be taken figuratively. I started to write these books many years ago, but after making small progress, I became dissatisfied with my approach. For I noticed if I were to expound on these passages by means of allegorical and mystical expressions, I would not accomplish anything. All I would be doing, would be to substitute one thing for another of the same kind. And if I were to explain them fully, the masses [who could not understand] would take a dim view of my effort. After all, my objective in writing these books was to explain the contents of the Midrashim and the prophetic revelations to the masses. If a simple rabbi reads these Midrashim, he will not find them difficult at all; since an empty mind that does not recognize the reality of things will not reject impossible things. When an intelligent and devout person reads them, if he takes them at face value he will think the writer [of the Midrash] incompetent and will not negate the principles of our faith, and if not he realizes that the passages in question have hidden meaning, and will continue to think highly of the author, whether he understands the allegory or not.

Because of these reasons I laid aside writing these books. In my larger work, Mishneh Torah, I limited myself to writing a brief summary of the principles of our faith and its fundamental truths. In this work, however, I address those who have studied philosophy, have a solid background in the sciences, and who, although they firmly believe in the principles of the Torah, are perplexed and bewildered by the words in Tanach with various metaphorical and figurative meanings. In this work we give a limited explanation of prophecy and its various levels and the different metaphors used in the books of the Prophets. Some chapters in this book contain no mention of words with multiple meanings, but serve as introductions to other chapters.

Having spoken about allegories, I wish to make the following points: The key to clear comprehension of the words of the Prophets is found in understanding the allegories, their intent and the meaning of each word they contain. You are familiar with the verse, *"I spoke parables through the prophets"* (Hoshea 12:11), and with the verse, *"Put forth a riddle and relate an allegory"* (Yechezkel 17:2). Because the Prophets regularly use parables, Yechezkel describes a prophet as one *"who speaks in parables"* (Yechezkel 21:5). Then there are the opening words of Mishlei, *"For understanding proverb and figurative speech, the words of the wise and their riddles"* (Mishlei 1:6). In Midrash it says, "To what were the words of the Torah compared before the time of Shlomoh? To a well whose waters were refreshingly cool but very deep and no one could drink from them. A clever man came and tied a cord to a cord and a rope to a rope, drew water and drank. So did Shlomoh go from parable to parable and from one topic to another until he crystallized the true meaning of the Torah *(Shir Hashirim Rabbah 1:1)*." I do not think that any intelligent person believes that when the Midrash says that *the meaning of the Torah was crystallized by means of parables,* it refers to the rules for building a *sukkah,* for preparing the *lulav* or the laws regarding the four kinds of custodians. What the Midrash means is the clear comprehension of profound and complex subjects. Our Sages said about such subjects, "If a person loses a *sela* (a large coin) or a pearl in his house, he can find it by lighting a candle worth one *issar* (a small coin). So too, the parables themselves are not worth much, but through the parables the words of the Torah become easy to understand."

Think about this. The deeper significance of the words of the Torah are the pearls, the literal interpretation of the allegory is meaningless. The Midrash compares the underlying meaning of the allegory to a pearl lost in a dark room full of furniture. It is certain the pearl is in the room, but the man cannot see it and does not know where it is. It is as if the pearl is no longer in his possession, for he cannot use it until he lights a candle. It is the same with the comprehension of the idea the allegory represents.

THE STRUCTURE OF A FIGURE OF SPEECH

The wise King Shlomoh said, "*Like golden apples in silver perforated ornamental network, so is a phrase well turned.*" Look how wonderfully this simile meets the criteria of a good figure of speech! Which is, whenever a word has a double meaning—a literal one and a figurative one—the literal meaning must be like silver, and the underlying meaning must be more precious—it must be like gold. It is also necessary that the literal sense of the phrase should convey the idea of its underlying meaning. In the case of the present simile—*the golden apple covered by a network of silver*—if you see it from a distance, or merely glance at it, you mistake it for a silver apple. But a sharp-eyed person looking at it discovers the apple is gold. The same is true with allegories used by the Prophets. If you take them literally, they contain wisdom used for many purposes, including advice for the advancement of human society. You can see this in their proverbs [like Mishlei and Koheles] when taken in their literal sense. But their underlying meaning contains wisdom helpful in recognizing the essence of Truth.

TWO TYPES OF BIBLICAL ALLEGORIES

The Prophets use two kinds of metaphors: first, where every word of the simile represents a certain idea; and second, where the simile, taken as a whole, represents a general idea, but has many points having nothing to do with the idea; they are there simply to hold the simile together and give it structure, or to hide the idea better. The simile is continued as far as necessary, according to its literal sense. Keep this in mind.

An example of the first category of prophetic allegories is Yaakov's vision in a dream, *"A ladder was standing on the ground, and its top reached up toward heaven. God's angels were going up and down on it. Suddenly he saw God standing over him"* *(Bereishis 28:12)*. The word *ladder* refers to one idea, *standing on the ground* to another, *and its top reached to heaven* to a third, *God's angels* to a fourth, *going up* to a fifth, *and going down* to a sixth, *God standing over him* to a seventh. Every word in this allegory adds a novel idea to the subject that is represented by the allegory. [See Chapter 15 for the explanation of this].

An example of the second category of prophetic allegories is found in Mishlei, where it says,

"From the window of my house, through my lattice I looked out, and saw among the simple, noticed among the youths, a lad devoid of sense. He was crossing the street near her corner, walking toward her house, in the dusk of evening in the dark hours of the night. A woman comes toward him, dressed like a harlot, with set purpose. She is bustling and restless, she is never at home. Now in the street, now in the square, she lurks at every corner. She lays hold of him and kisses him, brazenly she says to him, 'I had to bring a peace offering; today I fulfilled my vows. Therefore, I have come out to you, seeking you, and I have found you. I have decked my couch with covers of dyed Egyptian linen. I have sprinkled my bed with myrrh, aloes, and cinnamon. Let us drink our fill of love till morning, let us delight in amorous embrace. For the man of the house is away; he is off on a distant journey. He took his bag of money with him and will return only at mid-month.' She sways him with her eloquence, turns him aside with her smooth talk. Thoughtlessly he follows her, like an ox going to the slaughter, like a fool to the stocks for punishment.

Until the arrow pierces his liver. He is like a bird running into the trap, not knowing his life is at stake. Now, sons, listen to me; pay attention to my words. Let your mind not wander down her ways; do not stray onto her paths. For many are those she has struck dead, and numerous are her victims" (Mishlei 7:6-26).

The moral of these verses is to abstain from running after bodily pleasures and sensual delights. The author compares the physical world which is the source of all hedonistic pleasures to a harlot who is a married woman. He took this figure of speech as the basis of the entire book. In future chapters I will explain Shlomoh's wisdom in comparing sensual pleasures to an adulterous harlot. I will point out how fittingly he concludes Mishlei with the praises of the faithful wife who devotes herself to the welfare of her husband and household. All hindrances, shortcomings and rebellious tendencies preventing man from attaining the ultimate perfection, are due to his physical nature, as I will explain in this book.

The consistent thread running through the above-mentioned allegory is that a person should not solely follow his animal instincts which is his material nature. For the physical aspect of man is almost the same as that of the animal world, [both possess the life force, the only difference being man's soul which is manifest in his ability to think and speak].

Now that I explained to you the meaning of the allegory, don't expect to find a matching moral for each part of the allegory. Don't ask what is meant by *I had to bring a peace offering* by *I have decked out my couch with covers* or what idea is contributed by *For the man of the house is away* and so on to the end of the chapter. All this is merely to round off the background of the imagery, all the details mentioned are part of the environment of adulterers. Such conversations take place between adulterous persons. Understand clearly what I said, for it is a fundamental principle with regard to the things that I want to explain. If you notice in one of the chapters in this book that I explain the meaning of a certain allegory or parable, and point out the moral of the allegory, don't go looking for an interpretation of each component of that allegory, that would lead you astray in one of the following two ways: either you will miss the intended moral of the allegory, or you waste time trying to explain things that have no meaning, and need no explanation. Your unnecessary efforts will lead you to make the grave error that affects most present-day circles of thinkers. They all try to find some hidden significance in sayings never meant in that sense by the author. In most allegories you should try to discover the general idea the author wants to convey. In some cases be satisfied when I say that a certain passage is meant to be taken figuratively, although I offer no further comment. For when you understand that it should not be taken literally, you will gather at once the underlying idea it refers to. By saying that a certain verse is a figurative expression it is enough to remove the screen from between the observer and the object to be viewed.

INSTRUCTIONS FOR STUDYING THIS WORK

If you want to understand the contents of this book without missing anything, study the chapters in consecutive order. When you are studying a chapter, don't settle for merely understanding its subject matter but focus on every word, even though it may have no bearing on the subject. I did not write this work off the top of my head; it was written with meticulous care and the utmost vigilance. I saw to it that nothing that seemed doubtful should be left unexplained. Nothing is out of place, [and if you do find comments that seem to be out of context], this was done in order to clarify the subject matter of that chapter. Don't just skim over its pages, because you would hurt me, and would derive no benefit for yourself. Study thoroughly and reflect on it continuously, for then you will find answers to those basic problems of religion that every thinking person wonders about. I appeal to any reader of my book, in the name of Almighty, not to add even a single word to any explanation, nor to explain any part of it to someone else, except for passages that have been fully expounded by previous authorities. He may not teach others anything he learned from my book alone, which has not been discussed by our Sages. The reader should be careful not to contradict my statements, because it is quite likely that he understands my words to mean the exact opposite of what I intended to say. He will do me harm, while I tried to help him. He will be repaying good with evil. Let the reader study this book to the best of his ability, if he finds an answer for even one question that tormented him, let him praise Hashem and be happy with what he learned. But if this book is of no benefit to him, he should put it out of his mind and make believe it was never written. If he comes across any opinions with which he does not agree, let him try to find an acceptable explanation, even if it is far-fetched, and let him judge me favorably. That is a duty we owe to everyone. We owe it especially to our scholars and Torah Sages who teach us the truth as best they can.

Those of my readers who have not studied philosophy will derive benefit from some of the chapters. But a religious intellectual who is perplexed, as I mentioned earlier, will gain a great deal from every chapter. How happy will he be! How pleased will he be to hear my words! However, people who are confused, and whose minds have been warped with false doctrines and erroneous methods, who consider their misleading theories as science and think of themselves as philosophers although they have no knowledge of the genuine, will disagree with many chapters. They will find them beyond their comprehension because they do not understand their meaning, and because I expose in them the fallacy of their fraudulent doctrines which they consider their riches and beloved treasure but which in reality is their downfall. When I have a difficult subject before me, when I find the road narrow and can see no other way of teaching a proven fact except by pleasing one intelligent person and displeasing ten thousand fools, I would rather speak to that one man and disregard the scorn of the multitude. I would rather free that intelligent man from his predicament and show him the cause of his perplexity, so he may attain perfection and gain inner peace.

Hashem knows I hesitated very much before I wrote the topics contained in this work, since they are deep mysteries. They are subjects about which no books have been written by anyone since the time of our exile. How then shall I begin and commit them to writing? But I relied on two precedents: First, in similar cases, our Sages applied the verse, *"It is a time to act for Hashem, for they have violated your Torah"* (Tehillim 119:126).[3] Second, the Sages said, *"Let all your deeds be for the sake of Heaven"* (Avos 2:12). I relied on these two principles when composing some of the chapters of this work.

---

3. When the survival of the Torah is at stake we must violate the laws of the Torah in order to save the Torah. If not for the Rambam's *Moreh Nevuchim*, his entire generation would have fallen prey to the false doctrines of the contemporary philosophers.

CHAPTER 1

THE MEANING OF צלם—*IMAGE*, תואר—*FORM* AND דמות—*LIKENESS*

People used to think that the Hebrew word צלם *image* denoted the image and shape of a thing. As a result, they thought of Hashem as a physical, tangible Being. Hashem said, *"Let us make man with our image" (Bereishis 1:26)* which they understood to mean "with our figure and shape." This led them to the conclusion that He had a bodily form, and they accepted it. Indeed they thought if they were to give up this idea they would be rejecting the truth as stated in the Torah. What's more, they thought if they did not imagine Hashem having a body with a clearly defined face and hands, just as they, they would be guilty of denying His very existence. They did recognize, that Hashem was larger and brighter, and that His substance was not flesh and blood. This sums up their notion of the magnificence of Hashem.

The concept of Hashem's non-physical nature and His absolute Oneness—and there can be no real Oneness in a physical entity—will be proved in detail later on in Chapter 46. In this chapter we will focus on explaining how the words *image* and *likeness* can be used in reference to Hashem.

THE MEANING OF תואר—*FORM*

The Hebrew term for *form*, in the conventional meaning of *the figure and shape of a thing*, is תואר. For example, it says, *"[Yosef was] beautiful in form, and beautiful in appearance"*

17

(Bereishis 39:6); and, *"What is* his *form?" (1 Shmuel 38:14),* meaning, *What does he look like?* and, *"As the form of the sons of a king," (Shofetim 8:18)* [meaning, "They looked like sons of a king."] The word *form* is also used to describe a form produced by human labor, as in, *"[The craftsman] marks its form with a line, and marks out its shape with a compass" (Yeshayah 44:13).* The term תואר *form,* because it always refers to physical form, does not apply to Hashem, Heaven forbid.

THE MEANING OF צלם—*IMAGE*

The word צלם *image,* however, denotes the natural form, meaning, the essence of the thing, the individuality by which it is what it is, the reality of the thing. In man, his *image* is his human intellect. Because of man's intellect, the Torah uses the word *image* in the verses, *"In the image of Hashem He created him' (Bereishis 1:27).* For the same reason it says, *"You despise their image" (Tehillim 73:20).* [David is praying that Hashem should despise the *image* of the wicked.] Hashem's loathing can only be directed at the soul of a person, not at the characteristics and the shape of his body. [Man's *image* is his soul and his intellect. Surely Hashem does not despise a person because of his physical appearance, if his character is upright.]

I think the reason why idols are called *images* is because they are worshipped for the idea they represent, not on account of their figure and shape. The word *image* is used in the verse, *"[The Philistines were to] make images (figures) of their hemorrhoids" (1 Shmuel 6:5),* because the Philistines' main purpose was to be cured of the hemorrhoids, [which is an idea], not to represent their shape.

THE MEANING OF דמות—*LIKENESS*

דמות is derived from the verb דמה *to be like, to resemble*. This word also suggests similarity with regard to an abstract factor, like in the verse, *"I am **like** a bird in the wilderness"* *(Tehillim 102:7)*. The author is not comparing himself to a bird for its wings and feathers, but likens his sorrow, [an abstract feeling] to the bird's sorrow. So too the verse, *"No tree in the garden of Hashem was **like it** in beauty"* *(Yechezkel 31:8)*. The comparison refers to the idea of beauty. Again, *"Their venom is **like** the venom of a snake"* *(Tehillim 58:5)* and, *"His appearance is **like** a lion"* *(Tehillim 17:12)*. The analogies in all these verses do not relate to figure and shape, rather to abstract ideas.

In this way we find *likeness* used in *"The likeness of the [Divine] Throne"* *(Yechezkel 1:26)*. The comparison here is to convey the magnificence and grandeur of Hashem, not, as many believe, the shape, width and length of the Divine Throne. The same is true of, *"the **likeness** of the fiery angels"* *(Yechezkel 1:13)*.

Man has a unique faculty that sets him apart from all other creatures on earth, namely, his thinking mind. When a person thinks, he does not use his senses, he does not move his body, hands or legs. In that respect, it may seem—although it is not quite true—that man's power of abstract thinking is like Hashem's perception, for Hashem does not require any organs for perception. With respect to man's God-given power to think the Torah says he has been made in the *image* and *likeness* of Hashem. It should be clearly understood that Hashem does not have a physical body, material image or form.

CHAPTER 2

—◦◉◦—

THE LEVEL OF ADAM
BEFORE HE SINNED

A number of years ago, a learned man asked me a fundamental question. Ponder his question and the solution we offered. But before we go into this issue and its solution, I want to say, every Jew knows that the word אלהים *Elohim* has a number of different meanings. It refers to Hashem, angels, judges, and rulers of countries. Onkelos, the convert [in his Targum Onkelos] translated it correctly in the verse, *"[The serpent said to the woman: Your eyes will be opened,] and you will be like Elohim"* (Bereishis 3:5). He rendered *Elohim* according to the last-mentioned meaning, translating the phrase as, *you will be like rulers.* Now that we have pointed out that *Elohim* has several different meanings, let us turn our attention to the question at hand.

A KEY QUESTION

The questioner asked, "On the surface, as I read the Torah account of Creation, [which relates that after Adam ate from the forbidden Tree of Knowledge he became able to distinguish between good and evil,] it seems that man was originally meant to be just like the other animals, a creature without intellect and reason, unable to distinguish between good and evil. But by transgressing Hashem's command, man earned the great perfection which makes him unique, namely, the power to discern between good and evil, the most admirable of all our qualities, the essential attribute that gives man his self-awareness. Now, isn't it strange that the punishment for his disobedience should be to receive his intellect and be lifted to a level of perfection he had not attained before? This amounts to saying someone was rebellious and behaved badly, in return they changed his nature for the better, and was made a shining star in the sky."

Basically, this is the gist and the intent of the question, although not in the exact words of the questioner. Now take note of our reply.

THE RAMBAM'S ANSWER

[The Rambam admonishes the questioner:] You admit you glanced at the subject matter superficially, yet you think you understand [The Torah], a book that has been the guiding light of past and present generations. You skimmed over its pages during spare moments while eating and drinking as though reading a history book or some lyrical poem. If you consider the matter and give it some thought, you will realize [that originally man was not meant to be the same as all animals], as you thought at first glance. After serious consideration you will discover that the intellect that Hashem bestowed on Adam as the peak of his perfection was given to him before his transgression. The Torah has this intellect in mind when it says that man was created *in the image and likeness of Hashem*. It was because of his intellect that Hashem spoke to Adam and gave him His commandment, as it says, *"Hashem gave Adam a commandment" (Bereishis 2:16).* No commandments were given to the beasts or to those who [as yet] have no understanding. Through his intellect man can tell the difference between truth and falsehood, and Adam possessed this capacity to the fullest.

ADAM HARISHON BEFORE HIS TRANSGRESSION

Right and wrong are value concepts that are applicable to the mundane world [which is the realm of morality], not to the world of absolute truths. For example, you cannot say that the statement *the heavens are spherical* is good, or the contention that *the earth is flat* is bad. But you can say one is true and the other false. In our language we use the terms אמת *true* and שקר *false* for that which is intrinsically *true* or *false* and the terms טוב *good* and רע *bad* for what is morally *good* and morally *bad*. Man can distinguish between truth and falsehood by using his intellect—and he can apply this distinction to all transcendent ideas.

When Adam was in his state of perfection [before his transgression] his mind was totally absorbed in celestial thoughts and lofty ideas, because of that it says about him, *"You made him slightly less than the angels" (Tehillim 8:6).* [Since he was entirely immersed in otherworldly thoughts], the rules and principles of the mundane world were completely foreign to him, to the point that he saw nothing wrong with appearing in a state of nakedness, the most blatant form of indecency. He could not understand why this should be improper. But as soon as he began to think about transgressing, [although he had not yet actually sinned], he was swayed by his physical desire and the wish to seek sensual pleasure, as it says, *"The tree was good to eat and desirable to the eyes" (Bereishis 3:6).* He was punished by losing his faculty of thinking only otherworldly, ethereal, thoughts. As a result of this lost faculty he transgressed the commandment [not to eat from the Tree of Knowledge] given to him because he had an intellect. He now attained knowledge of the mundane world and sank to the level where he had to deal with moral right and wrong. At that point he realized what a tremendous loss he suffered, what had been taken from him, and to what a low level he fell.

That is why it says, [when referring to the results of eating from the Tree of Knowledge] *"You will be like Elohim, knowing good and evil"* (Bereishis 3:4) and it does not say, *knowing truth and falsehood,* or, *differentiating between truth and falsehood.* [Thus the answer to the questioner's query is: Before Adam's sin—before he learned to distinguish between good and evil—he possessed the far superior faculty of thinking only otherworldly thoughts which was taken from him when he sinned.] When it comes to [timeless and unchanging] realities we can only speak in terms of *true and false,* not *good and evil.*

Now consider the passage, *"The eyes of both of them were opened, and they realized they were naked"* (ibid. 7). [Note, it says, *and they realized.*] It does not say, "The eyes of both of them were opened, *and they saw,*" because what they had seen before the transgression was exactly the same as what they saw afterwards. It was not that Adam had been blind [before the sin], and now this blindness was removed. Rather, he received a new awareness through which he found things wrong, which before the sin he had not considered wrong.

In this connection, you should know that the verb פקח *to open,* is used only in the sense of opening the mind to receive new knowledge; [the phrase, *their eyes were opened*] certainly does not mean that Adam was given the sense of sight. Compare also, *"God opened her eyes"* (Bereishis 21:19); *"Then shall the eyes of the blind be opened"* (Yeshayah 38:8); *"With ears open, he hears nothing"* (ibid. 42:20), which is similar in meaning to the verse, *"They have eyes to see but see not"* (Yechezkel 12:2). [In all these verses the opening of the eyes is meant in a figurative sense, as *gaining new knowledge*].

When you read about Adam, *"He [Adam] changed his face, and You sent him away"* (Iyov 14:20), [don't take this literally and infer that his physical face was changed and he received the capability to see.] What it means is this: He was sent away because he turned away from his original aim. For the word פנים—*face*, is derived from the verb פנה—*to turn*, because a person will usually turn his face in the direction of his aim. Thus, when Adam changed his aim and made up his mind to do the thing that he was told not to do, he was expelled from the Garden of Eden. This punishment was given measure for measure. Originally he was permitted to partake of pleasure and enjoy tranquility and security. But when his cravings grew stronger, and he began running after physical delights he ate the things he was forbidden to eat, everything [i.e. his clear and unobscured intellect] was taken away from him. He was doomed to eat the most mediocre food, such as he had never tasted before, and even this only after arduous labor and a great deal of exertion. As it says, *"[The earth] will bring forth thorns and thistles for you. . . By the sweat of your brow you will eat bread" (Bereishis 3:18,19).* Elaborating on this, the text continues, *"Hashem banished [man] from the Garden of Eden, to work the ground from which he was taken." (ibid. 3:24).* With regard to his food and bodily needs he was reduced to the level of an animal, as it says, *"You will eat the grass of the field" (ibid. 18).* Reflecting on the precariousness of the human condition the Psalmist says, *"Adam was unable to abide in glory, he was brought down to the level of a dumb animal" (Tehillim 49:13).* [Even Adam, God's handiwork, sinned and fell from his pinnacle on the very day he was created.]

May the Almighty be praised whose ultimate plan and wisdom cannot be fathomed.

CHAPTER 3

———≈◉≈———

The Meaning of תבנית—*Shape* and תמונה—*Picture*

You may think the Hebrew words תבנית *shape* and תמונה *picture* have the same meaning, but this is not so. תבנית *shape,* a noun derived from the verb בנה, *to build,* denotes the build and structure of a thing, its pattern or shape, whether it is square, round, triangular, or other contour. And so it says, *"the **pattern** of the Tabernacle and the pattern of all its furnishings"* (Shemos 25:9); *"according to the **pattern** that you will be shown on the mountain"* (ibid. 40). *"the **shape** of any bird"* (Devarim 4:17); *"the **shape** of a hand"* (Yechezkel 8:3); *"the **pattern** of the porch"* (1 Divrei Hayamim 28:11). In all these quotations pattern and shape refer to physical pattern and shape. Therefore the Hebrew language never uses the word תבנית when speaking of Hashem.

תמונה—*Picture*

The word תמונה *picture,* on the other hand, is used in Tanach, with three different meanings. First, it denotes the outlines of things that can be perceived by our physical senses, as in *"and you will make for yourself a statue a **picture** of some visible form"* (Devarim 4:16); *"for you saw no **picture*** (Devarim 4:15). Secondly, the word *picture* signifies the forms of our imagination, i.e. the impressions of events that remain in our mind after they passed from the scene and cannot be perceived by our senses. In this sense the term *picture* is used in the passage which begins, *"In thought-filled visions of the night,"* and which ends, *"It remained, its appearance was strange to me, only a **picture** loomed before my eyes" (Job 4:13,16)*. What Job means to say is that an image appeared before his eyes while he was asleep. Thirdly, [תמונה *picture* denotes] the true essence of an object which is perceived only by the intellect. It is in this third connotation that the word *picture* is applied to God. Therefore, when it says, *"And he (Moshe) beholds the **picture** of Hashem" (Bamidbar 12:8)*, it means, *he comprehends the true essence of Hashem.*

CHAPTER 4

THE MEANING OF ראה—*SEE*, הביט—*LOOK* AND חזה—*GAZE*

The three verbs, ראה—*see*, הביט—*Look* and חזה—*gaze*, refer to seeing with eyes. They are also used metaphorically in the sense of perceiving with the mind or understanding. Regarding the verb *to see*, everyone knows that it has these two meanings. For example, when it says, *"He saw a well in the field" (Bereishis 29:2)* it obviously means he literally saw the well with his eyes. And when it says, *"My mind has seen a great deal of wisdom and learning,"* it is clear this refers to intellectual perception.

Whenever the verb ראה *to see* is applied to Hashem it should be understood in the figurative sense, for example, *"I saw Hashem" (1 Melachim 22:19); "And Hashem appeared to him" (Bereishis 18:1); "And God saw that it was good*

*(Bereishis 1:10); "Please let me see Your glory" (Shemos 33:18);
"And they saw the God of Israel" (Shemos 24:10).* All these examples of man seeing Hashem refer to intellectual perception, not to seeing in the literal sense. For the eye can only
perceive a tangible object and only some of its features, like
the color and shape of the object [not even its texture or
whether it is hot or cold]. By the same token, when it says
God saw it is not by means of a physical organ, as will be explained [in chapter 44].

הביט—*LOOK*

The term הביט refers to looking at something with the eye,
like in the verse, *"Do not look back!" (Bereishis 19:17);
"[Lot's] wife looked behind him" (Bereishis 18:26); "And he
will look below" (Yeshayah 5:30).* It is also used metaphorically to signify *viewing with the intellect* and *pondering a concept
until you understand it.* In this sense the verb *look* is used in
the verse, *"[Hashem] does not look at wrongdoing in Yaakov"
(Bamidbar 23:21);* because *wrongdoing* cannot be seen with
the eye. The words, *"They would look at Moshe" (Shemos
33:8)*—in addition to their plain meaning—were explained
by the Sages in a metaphoric sense. They interpreted this
phrase to mean the Jewish people examined and probed the
actions and sayings of Moshe. Likewise, the phrase, *"Look at
the sky and count the stars" (Bereishis 15:5)* [does not refer to
visual sighting, but to intellectual perception] because it took
place in a prophetic vision [of Avraham]. Whenever the verb
look is applied to Hashem it is used in a figurative sense.

חזה—*To Gaze*

The same is true of the verb חזה—*to gaze*. It signifies *to view, to gaze with the eye*, as in, *"And let our eye gaze on Zion" (Michah 4:11);* and metaphorically, to perceive with the mind, as in, *"[The prophecy] which he viewed concerning Yehudah and Yerushalayim" (Yeshayah 1:1); "God's word came to Avraham in a vision (Bereishis 15:1).* It is in this figurative sense that it is used referring to Hashem as in *"They viewed God" (Shemos 24:11).* Keep this in mind.

CHAPTER 5

THE REQUIREMENTS FOR THE KNOWLEDGE OF THE DIVINE

When [Aristotle], the foremost philosopher, set out to explore a very profound subject and substantiate his theories by proofs, he began his discourse with an apology. He asked readers of his work not to accuse him of audacity, boastfulness, conceit, or arrogance for delving into subjects he knew nothing about. He asked them to understand that he was motivated by diligence and driven by a strong desire to discover and confirm true beliefs as much as humanly possible.

I want to make the same apology. I think when a person begins to research a subject as vast and as profound [as the knowledge of Hashem and His manifestation on Mount Sinai] he should not rush headlong into it. He should first familiarize himself with the basics of Divine science and knowledge, then he should very thoroughly refine his character traits and subdue his lusts and desires which stem from his imagination. When he knows and understands the fundamental principles of logic, has a grasp of the various methods of comparison and proof, and is capable of guarding against faulty reasoning, then he may advance to the stage where he can explore the subject [of knowledge of Hashem]. But he should not decide any issue by the first idea that springs up in his mind, or immediately focus all his thoughts on gaining an understanding of the Creator. Rather, he should restrain himself [from delving into things that are beyond human comprehension], wait humbly [until he is ready to study the things that are within human reach], and advance one step at a time.

This was Moshe's attitude [when Hashem appeared to him for the first time in the thorn-bush], as it says, *"Moshe hid his face, because he was afraid to look at the Divine"* *(Shemos 3:6)*. The plain meaning is that Moshe was afraid to gaze at the light shining in his eyes. But don't think for a moment that Hashem Who is exalted far above any imperfection can be perceived by the eye. [The passage means that Moshe humbly restrained himself from seeking knowledge of Hashem.]

Hashem praised Moshe for this act, and bestowed on him a richly deserved share of His goodness, as it says, *"He (Moshe) beholds a likeness of Hashem"* *(Bamidbar 12:8)*. According to our Sages *(Berachos 7a)*, this was his reward for hiding his face and not looking at Hashem.

THE ERROR OF THE LEADERS OF ISRAEL

But the leaders of Israel were impulsive and gave free rein to their thoughts. [They did not humbly restrain themselves as

Moshe did, therefore when they perceived the Divine, it was an imperfect perception.] That's why it says about them, *"They saw a vision of the God of Israel, and under His feet ..."* *(Shemos 24:10)*, and not simply, *They saw a vision of the God of Israel.* The phrase [*and under his feet*] is a veiled criticism of their act of seeing; it does not describe what they saw, rather the leaders are being faulted for the nature of their vision which included an element of corporeality, [i.e. the feet of God]. Their imperfect, blurred vision came as a result of their being overanxious and reaching for Divine knowledge before they were ready. For this they deserved to die. But in response to Moshe's prayer Hashem relented and postponed their sentence. Later most of them were consumed by fire at Taveirah (Bamidbar 11:1-3), and Nadav and Avihu died by fire in the Tabernacle, (Vayikra 10:2) according to the Midrash on these verses.

Now, if this was [what happened to the leaders], then certainly we who are inferior, and surely those inferior to us, have the duty to apply ourselves and concentrate on perfecting our knowledge of the underlying principles and on understanding the primary propositions that cleanse the mind from the defilement of error; then we will be able to begin to view the holy and divine camp. As it says, *"The priests, who come near the Divine must also sanctify themselves, or else God will send destruction among them"* *(Shemos 19:22)*, [meaning, thinking people who want to study the knowledge of the Divine and understand His existence must prepare themselves by studying the preliminary basic lessons, otherwise their minds will be adversely affected, as happened to the leaders of Israel].

Shlomoh also strongly warned those who are trying to reach this sublime level of knowledge, in the following poetic admonition, *"Guard your foot when you go to the house of God"* *(Koheles 4:17)*.

I will now backtrack and finish what I began to explain. The faulty perception of the Divine by the leaders of Israel caused them to stumble in their actions. Their muddled vision of the Divine stirred in them a craving for bodily enjoyment. You can see this in the passage, *"They had a vision of the Divine, and they ate and drank" (Shemos 24:11).* For now, all I wish to say is, that wherever the verbs *to see, look* or *view* occur in relation to Hashem they refer to intellectual perception, not to seeing with the eye. For Hashem is not a being that can be perceived by the eye.

It will do no harm, however, if someone who is unable to understand what I am trying to explain, in this instance interprets these words as referring to actual sight with the eyes, and will explain that they saw a light which was a manifestation of the Shechinah or the angels.

CHAPTER 6

---◈---

THE MEANING OF איש—*MAN*
AND אשה—*WOMAN*

The two nouns איש—*man* and אשה—*woman* were originally used to indicate the male and the female of human beings. Afterwards they were applied to the male and female of the other species of the animal world. For example, it says, *"Take seven pairs of every clean animal, each consisting of a man and his woman, (mate)" (Bereishis 7:2),* in the same sense as, *male and female.* Later on, the term *woman* or *female* was applied to anything meant to be joined to something else. And so it says, "*The five tapestries shall be cou-pled together, a **woman** to her **sister** (Shemos 26:3),* [meaning one to another.]

It is obvious that the terms אחות—*sister* and אח—*brother* are also used both in a literal and in a figurative sense, like man and women.

CHAPTER 7

THE MEANING OF ילד—*GIVE BIRTH*

It is known that the plain meaning of the verb ילד is *to bear, to father, to give birth to* as in, "*they **bore** him sons*" *(Devarim 21:15)*. Later the word was used metaphorically in the sense of *to create* with reference to various things in nature. For example, "*Before the mountains were **born** (creat-ed)*" *(Tehillim 90:2)*; also in the sense of *to sprout, to bring forth* in relation to the things the earth produces, as in "*He will cause [the earth] to **bear** (bring forth) and sprout vegeta-tion*" *(Yeshayah 55:10)*. The verb *to bear* also signifies *to bring* relative to changes in time, as if events were things that were born, for example, "*For you do not know what the day will **bear** (bring)*" *(Mishlei 27:1)*. To bear is also used to describe the creation of new ideas, or opinions that arise from them, as in, "*he gives **birth** to fraud*" *(Tehillim 7:15)*; also, "*and they take pleasure in the **children** of aliens*" *(Yeshayah 2:6)*, mean-ing, *they delight in alien ideas*. Yonasan ben Uziel (Targum Yonasan) interprets this passage, *they walk in the customs of other nations*.

ADAM'S SON SHES

[According to this last interpretation,] if a person taught someone, he may be considered his father, because the teacher created the knowledge in the student. That is why the disciples of the prophets are called *sons of prophets.*

The verb ילד—*to bear* is used in this figurative sense in the verse, "*And Adam lived 130 years, and he produced a son in his likeness and form*" *(Bereishis 1:3).* Those sons of Adam born before [he reached the age of 130], were not really human; they did not have the likeness and form of Adam which was "*the likeness and form of God.*" They did not achieve a level of intellect comparable to Adam. But Shes [the son who was born to Adam when he was 130 years old] was taught and enlightened by Adam and brought to the peak of human perfection. About him it can rightly be said *[Adam] produced a son in his likeness and form.*

A DESCRIPTION OF BARBARIC PEOPLE

It is well known that a person who does not have this [Divine] *form*—[who did not develop his intellect]—is not human, but merely an animal in human form. A [formless] creature like this has the power to cause untold harm and devise all kinds of appalling atrocities. No other animal has such power. For he does not use the intelligence and thinking power that he received in order to attain moral perfection. Instead, he uses these gifts to invent ways of inflicting harm and causing destruction. [He is not human;] but merely resembles man and impersonates him. This was nature of the sons of Adam that were born before Shes. Speaking about this subject the Midrash says, "During the 130 years that Adam was under God's reprimand he generated spirits, i.e.

demons; but when Hashem accepted him again in His favor he *produced a son in his likeness and his form.* This is the meaning of the passage, *"Adam lived 130 years, and he **produced** a son in his likeness and form."*[1]

CHAPTER 8

————◦◉◦————

THE MEANING OF מקום—*PLACE*

The primary definition of the word מקום—*place* is a point or portion of space. Later on its meaning was expanded, and it is now used to describe a person's position or status in a certain field. We say, for example: This person occupies a certain *position* in such and such an enterprise. It is well known that authors use the term *place* in the metaphoric sense. They say, for example, *He fills his ancestors' place in wisdom and fear of God.* And they use the expression, *the dispute still remains in its place* meaning *it is unreconcilable. Place* is used in a figurative sense in the verse, *"Blessed is the glory of Hashem from His place* "(Yechezkel 3:12). In this context *place* refers to the particular position or level of eminence of His existence. Wherever *place* is applied to God, it conveys the lofty level of His existence, which is incomparable and unequalled.

Bear in mind when we discuss words with multiple meanings, we do not limit you to what is mentioned in that chapter, but we open a gate and point out those meanings of the

---

1. The Shem Tov, a commentary on Moreh Nevuchim, notes: Pay close attention to this paragraph because it is extraordinary.It contains important allusions to events of the past the present and the future.

word that serve our purpose, although it is by no means a complete list from a linguistic point of view. Examine the Books of the Prophets and other works written by men of wisdom, notice the meaning of every word and choose the meaning that fits the context. What I say in a particular passage is a key to understanding all similar passages. For example, I have explained here *place* in the verse, "*Blessed is the glory of Hashem from His place*;" but understand the word place has the same meaning in the verse, "*See, there is a place near Me*" *(Shemos 33:21)*, meaning, *There is a way of reaching Me, through contemplation,* not through visual sighting. In addition, it has the literal meaning of a *place*, i.e. the mountain pointed out to Moshe where he should go into seclusion for the attainment of perfection.

CHAPTER 9

THE MEANING OF כסא—*THRONE*

Everyone knows the simple definition of כסא—*throne*. Now, since men of eminence and power, such as kings, sit on a throne, *the throne* has come to symbolize the stature, prominence and prestige [of the person who occupies it]. For that reason the *Beis Hamikdash* is also called *the throne*, since it represents the authority of the One who manifests Himself in it, and causes His light and glory to dwell in it. And so it says, "*O Throne of Glory, exalted from the beginning, is the place of our Beis Hamikdash,*" *(Yirmiyah 17:10)*. It is for the same reason that the heavens are called *throne*, to convey to the person who watches the sky and contemplates [the myriad heavenly bodies] the almightiness of Hashem who brought them into being, guides their orbits, and rules our lowly world with an abundant flow of goodness. And so it says, *"Thus says Hashem: The heavens are My throne and the earth is My footstool" (Yeshayah 66:1),* meaning, [the heavens] are proof of My Existence, My Essence, and My Omnipotence, just as a throne proves that its occupant is an illustrious personage.

True believers should bear this in mind; they should never think that Hashem is seated on a physical object. For Hashem has no physicality. This being so, how can it be said that He occupies space or rests on an object? I want to make this point: every place that was elevated by God and selected to receive His light and splendor, like, the *Beis Hamikdash* or the heavens, is called *throne.*

In the verse, *"The Hand is on God's Throne" (Shemos 17:16)* [which denotes a Divine oath], *Throne* is used figuratively, and stands for the Essence and Majesty of God. [Thus Hashem swears by His Essence and Majesty.] But don't think of [His Throne] as something other than Hashem Himself or as one of His creations, and say Hashem existed before the throne. Such a belief would undoubtedly be heresy. It says very clearly, *"But You, Hashem, remain forever; Your throne endures through the ages" (Eichah 5:19).* This proves that Hashem and His *Throne* are indivisible; [they are one and the same]. It should be noted that in this verse and all similar verses, the word *throne* stands for God's Majesty and Essence, which are inseparable from His Being. I will elaborate on this theme in future chapters.

CHAPTER 10

———◆———

THE MEANING OF ירד—*DESCEND*
AND עלה—*ASCEND*

We mentioned already that when we deal in this treatise with words having different meanings, we don't intend to mention all the variant meanings of that word. After all, this is not a dictionary. We mention only those meanings relevant to the subject at hand. Now we will examine the verbs ירד—*descend* and עלה—*ascend*.

The meaning of the two verbs, *descend* and *ascend* are known to everyone. When a body moves from a higher to a lower place we say, *he descended*. When it moves from a lower to a higher place we say, *he went up*. These two verbs were later used in a metaphoric sense in relation to greatness and power. When a person falls from a high position, we say, *he descended* and when he rises in stature we say, *he ascended*. And so Hashem says, *"The alien among you will rise higher and higher over you, while you will descend . . ."* (*Devarim 28:43*). And it says, *"Hashem will make you highest of all the nations on earth"* (*Devarim 28:1*), *"God made Shlomoh exceedingly **high** (great)"* (*1 Divrei Hayamim 24:25*). You know of course the expression of the Sages, "We may raise an object to a higher degree of sanctity but we may not lower it" (*Berachos 28a*). The two words are also applied to the thinking process. When a person speculates about a very down-to-earth concept he is said to have descended, when he meditates about lofty ideas he is said to ascend.

We humans are all on a very low level both regarding where we are and what we are in comparison with the heavenly sphere; and Hashem is the Most High, not in terms of space but with regard to absolute existence, greatness and power. Now, when Hashem desired it, He bestowed a measure of Divine wisdom and prophetic inspiration on a prophet. The prophecy that came to rest on the prophet, or the *Shechinah* dwelling in a certain place, is described as *descending*, whereas the end of the prophetic message or the departure of the *Shechinah* from a place is called *ascending*.[2]

Whenever the expressions *ascend* or *descend* are used in relation to God interpret them in this [metaphoric] sense. When it was God's will that a natural disaster should strike a nation or a region, and this disaster was predicted in a Biblical prophecy, the prophet called this Divine involvement [in the affairs of the world] a descent. For man is so lowly and inferior that, were it not God's will, his actions would not be worth punishing. This idea is clearly expressed in Tehillim, where it says, *"What is frail man that You should remember him, and the son of mortal man that You should be mindful of him?" (Tehillim 8:5)*.

Whenever the Torah tells us that Hashem intends to bring punishment on man, the verb *descend* is used. And so it says, [when Hashem spoke to the angels] *"Come let us **descend** and confuse their speech" (Bereishis 11:7)*; and *"Hashem **descended** to see the city and the tower" (ibid. 5); "I will **descend** and see" (ibid. 21)*. All these examples convey the idea that corrupt people are about to be punished.

However, there are many instances where *to descend* is used in connection with prophecy and the manifestation of the glory of Hashem. For example, *"And I will **come down** and I will talk to you there" (Bamidbar 11:17); "And Hashem **came down** on Mount Sinai" (Shemos 19:20); "Hashem will **come down** on Mount Sinai in the sight of all people" (ibid.*

---

2. When Hashem becomes manifest to lowly humans we consider it a descent on his part, and when he takes leave of lowly man we refer to Him as ascending.

*11); "And Hashem **went up** from him" (Bereishis 35:13); "And Hashem **went up** from Avraham" (ibid. 17:22).* On the other hand, when it says, *"And Moshe **ascended** to Hashem" (Shemos 19:3)* it must be understood in the sense that Moshe, through meditation, received prophetic inspiration. This is in addition to its literal meaning that Moshe physically climbed up the mountain on which a certain material light descended. It should be clearly understood that Hashem does not occupy a place to which a person can ascend, or from which he can descend. He is far removed from what ignorant people imagine Him to be.

CHAPTER 11

THE MEANING OF ישב—*SIT*

The primary definition of the verb ישב is *to sit*, as in the verse, *"The priest Eli was sitting on the seat" (1 Shmuel 1:9).* Now, since a person is more at rest when he is sitting than when standing, the term was applied to everything that is enduring and unchanging. And so, in the prophetic promise that Yerushalayim will remain forever in an exalted state, it says, *"She (Yerushalayim) will rise high up and **sit** in her place" (Zechariah 14:10).* And furthermore, *"He transforms the barren wife to **sit** as a glad mother of children" (Tehillim 113:9),* meaning, Hashem makes her [state of motherhood] lasting and enduring.

In this sense [of permanence] the word is applied to Hashem. For example, *"But You, Hashem, will **sit** forever"*

(Eichah 5:19); "O You, Who **sit** *in the heavens" (Tehillim 123:1); "He Who* **sits** *in heaven" (ibid. 2:4),* which means, He Who is eternal, everlasting, and unchangeable, His Essence is unsusceptible of change. Since He is nothing but His Essence, He is immutable. Since there exists no relation between Him and anything beside Him, the concept of change does not apply to Him. This will be explained in a later chapter. He is changeless in every respect, as He explicitly declares, *"I, Hashem, have not changed" (Malachi 3:6);* meaning, that there is no change in Him whatsoever. The idea [of permanence and changelessness] is implied whenever the term *sitting* is mentioned with reference to Hashem.

The verb *sit* is also used in describing God's relations to transient material things. And so it says, *"It is He who sits above the circle of the earth" (Yeshayah 60:22),* meaning, He Who remains constantly and perpetually over the sphere of the earth; in other words, over the things that come into being in that sphere.

We also find *sitting* mentioned in the verse, *"Hashem sits upon the Flood" (Tehillim 29:10),* which means that although material things undergo changes and pass from the scene, no change occurs with respect to Hashem's relation to the earth. His relationship to each of the things that come into existence and perish is stable and permanent. You should be aware, therefore, that whenever the term *to sit* is applied to Hashem Yisbarach it is used in this sense.

CHAPTER 12

---◆◈◈◆---

THE MEANING OF קם—*STAND*

The verb קם—*to stand* is a word of many meanings. In one of its definitions it is the opposite of *to sit*, as in *"[Mordechai] did not rise or even stir for him"* (Esther 5:9). Furthermore, it denotes the confirmation or fulfillment of something, for example, *"May Hashem uphold His promise"* (1 Shmuel 1:23); *"The field of Efron stood as the uncontested property of Avraham"* (Bereishis 23:17); *"The house in the walled city shall stand"* (Vayikra 25:30); *"And the kingdom of Israel shall stand (be firmly established) in your hand"* (1 Shmuel 24:20). It is always in this sense that the verb is used with reference to Hashem, as in, *"'Now I will arise!' Hashem will say"* (Tehillim 12:6), which is the same as saying, *"Now I will fulfill My word and My promise for good or evil." "You will arise and show Zion mercy"* (ibid. 102:14), meaning, *You will fulfill what You have promised, which is, that You have mercy on Zion."*

Usually when a person makes up his mind to do something he gets up. Therefore, when we describe a person who decided to take action we use the expression *he rose*. For example, *"No one informs me when my own son has set my servant in ambush against me"* (1 Shmuel 22:8). In this way the word is used figuratively to denote the carrying out of a divine decree against a people condemned to extermination, as *"I will rise against the house of Yerovam with the sword"* (Amos 7:9); *"So He will rise against the house of evildoers"* (Yeshayah 31:2).

There are many verses that must be understood this way,

but let no one think for a moment that Hashem gets up or sits down—Heaven forbid that anyone should say such a thing! Our Sages have a saying for it, *In the world above there is neither sitting nor standing.*

CHAPTER 13

THE MEANING OF עמד—*STOOD*

The verb עמד—*stood* is a word that has several meanings. First of all it denotes *to stand upright,* as in, *"When he stood before Pharaoh (Bereishis 41:46); and, "Even if Moshe and Shmuel stood" (Yirmiyah 15:1); "He stood by them" (Bereishis 18:8).* עמד—*Stand* also signifies *to cease, to end* and *to interrupt* as in, *"till they stood (ended) and no longer replied" (Iyov 32:16); "she stood from (stopped) having children" (Bereishis 29:35).* Furthermore, it means *to last, to endure,* as in, *"so that they may stand (last) a long time" (Yirmiyah 32:14); "then you will be able to stand (survive)" (Shemos 18:23); "His fine flavor has stood (remained)" (Yirmiyah 48:11),* which means that it has remained unchanged; *"His righteousness stands (endures) forever" (Tehillim 111:3),* meaning, it is undying and infinite. Wherever the verb *stood* occurs with reference to Hashem it should be interpreted in the sense of *enduring, lasting.* Then there is the verse, *"On that day His feet will stand on the Mount of Olives" (Zechariah 14:4),* which means, *His causes, that is to say, the things He brings to pass, will remain in existence.* We will elaborate on this [in Chapter 28] when we discuss the various meaning of *foot*. The verb is used in the same sense when Hashem is speaking to Moshe, saying, *"You, however, must **stand** (remain) here with Me"* (Devarim 5:28), [indicating that Moshe would henceforth always remain on the level of prophecy]; and *"I stood between Hashem and you"* (ibid. 5:5), [meaning *I (Moshe) remained at a lofty level between Hashem and you.*]

CHAPTER 14

THE MEANING OF אדם—*MAN*

The word אדם—*man* which has various meanings is, first of all, the name of *Adam Harishon,* the first man. As the Torah states, the name Adam is derived from *adamah,*[3] *earth.* It also means *mankind,* as in *"My spirit will not continue to judge **adam** (mankind) forever"* (Bereishis 6:3). And, *"Who knows the spirit of the children of **adam** (man)"* (Koheles 3:19); *"the pre-eminence of **adam** (mankind) over beast is non-existent"* (ibid. 19). Adam also denotes *the masses, the common man,* as opposed to men of distinction, as in, *"Both **adam** (common man) and the sons of men [of distinction]"* (Tehillim 49:3).

It is in this third connotation that *adam* occurs in the verses, *"The sons of the men of stature saw the daughters of **adam** (the common man)"* (Bereishis 6:2); and *"But like **adam** (common men) you will die"* (Tehillim 82:7).

---

3. In Hebrew the word for earth is Adamah—man who was taken from earth was named Adam to reflect this.

CHAPTER 15

—————◈—————

THE MEANING OF נצב AND יצב—*STAND UPRIGHT*

Although the two words נצב and יצב have different roots, yet their meaning is the same in all their grammatical forms.

This word has several meanings: in some cases it signifies *to stand* or *to take one's place, to station oneself,* as in *"[The child's] sister **stationed** herself at a distance"* (Shemos 2:7); *"The kings of the earth take their **stand**"* (Tehillim 2:2); *"They came out and **stood** defiantly"* (Bamidbar 16:27). In other cases it suggests endurance and everlastingness, as in *"Your word **stands** firm in heaven"* (Tehillim 119:89), meaning, it remains forever.

YAAKOV'S VISION OF THE LADDER

Whenever the term *stand* refers to Hashem it should be understood in the sense [of permanence], as in, *"Suddenly [Yaakov] saw Hashem **standing** upon it"*[4] (Bereishis 28:13), which means that Hashem appeared to Yaakov as everlasting. *Upon it,* that is to say, on the ladder, whose top reached to heaven, while its lower end stood on the earth. Whoever wishes to climb up this ladder may do so; he will surely attain the knowledge of Him Who is at the top of the ladder, since He stays there forever. I want to emphasize that the passage, *"Suddenly he saw Hashem standing upon it"* [should not be

---

4. Yaakov had a dream of a ladder reaching to Heaven. The Torah relates that Hashem was standing on the ladder and angels were ascending and descending it.

taken literally, because Hashem is not a material Being], rather it should be understood in accordance with the above mentioned metaphor [that Hashem appeared to Yaakov as everlasting]. The *angels of God* who were going up the ladder symbolize the prophets. And we can cite the following passages where prophets are explicitly called angels, like, *"He sent an angel who took us out of Egypt" (Bamidbar 20:16)* [the reference is to Moshe], and, *"An angel of Hashem came up from Gilgal to Bochim" (Shofetim 2:1),* [where Onkelos translates *angel* in this verse as, *prophet*. According to the Sages the reference is to Pinchas.]

How fitting is the expression *[the angels] were going up and down on [the ladder]*. They went up before they came down![5] After a person has climbed the [spiritual] ladder and reached the lofty levels [of prophecy] he descends to the mundane world in order to apply the knowledge he gained to leading and teaching the people. This application of his knowledge is called, *coming down*, as we explained.

CHAPTER 16

---•◦•---

THE MEANING OF צור—*ROCK*

The word צור—*rock* has several meanings. Its basic meaning is *rock*, as in, *"You must strike the rock" (Shemos 17:6)*. It also denotes *hard stone*, as in, *"Make knives of rock (flint)" (Yehoshua 5:2)*. Also the word *rock* is used for the quarry

---

5. This is proof that the *angels* referred to here are human prophets who begin their journey at the bottom of the ladder, not literal angels who would begin at the top.

from which the stones are cut, as in, *"Look to the rock you were hewn from" (Yeshayah 51:1)*. After that, the meaning of the word was broadened to signify the root and source of anything. That is why after the phrase, *"Look to the rock you were hewn from,"* the prophet continues, *"Look to Avraham your father,"* suggesting that the rock from which you were hewn was your father Avraham. The prophet means to say to the people: Follow in his ways, be faithful to his teachings and behave the way he did. For the characteristics of the quarry should be present in the things that are cut from it.

It is in the above mentioned sense [of *source* and *origin*] that Hashem is called *Rock,* for He is the beginning, the First Mover and the Cause of all things besides Himself. And so it says, *"The deeds of the Rock are perfect" (Devarim 32:4); "You thus ignored the Rock Who bore you" (ibid. 18); "Their Rock had sold them' (ibid. 31:30); "There is no rock like our God" (1 Shmuel 2:2); "The Rock of eternity" (Yeshayah 26:4)* and, *"You (Moshe) should stand on the rock" (Shemos 33:21)*. This should be taken idiomatically and rendered, "You must remain in contemplation that Hashem is the origin of all things," for this will lead you toward the knowledge of God.

This idea was also dealt with in chapter 8, when we discussed the verse, *"See, there is a place near Me"* [which was interpreted to mean, *There is a way of reaching up to Me.*]

CHAPTER 17

———◄◦►———

Do Not Teach Metaphysics to the General Public

D o not think metaphysics[6] is the only subject that should not be taught to the general public. The same is true of most natural sciences. We mentioned this in the introduction to this work, where we quoted the Mishnah, "Do not expound on the chapter of the Story of Creation in the presence of two" *(Chagigah 2:1)*. Not only did the Sages withhold this [esoteric] knowledge from the masses, ancient philosophers and scholars of other nations as well, used to keep the subject of the First Cause a dark secret and discussed such subjects using allusions and hints. For example, Plato and his predecessors called Substance[7] *the female,* and Form *the male.* You know that the three principal notions that govern all existing transitory things are: *Substance, Form* and *Absence.* Absence is always inherent in Substance, otherwise the substance would not be able to receive a new form.[8] That is why Absence is included among the three principal notions. As soon as the substance has received a certain form, the absence of that form has ended, but the absence of a future form takes its place, and so on forever [for substance

---

6. See footnote on page 3.

7. Substance *(chomer)*, Form *(tzurah)* and Absence *(headar)* are terms used by early philosophers and may be unfamiliar to the modern day reader. Substance is the permanent core underlying the fleeting qualities. Form is what gives pattern and character to everything. The form is also its final cause, its purpose and end.

8. Everything in nature perishes and takes on a new form. The individual who has passed maturity grows old and perishes *(Absence)*, but his form is carried on in his descendants undying into the future.

constantly takes on new forms], as explained in works on natural philosophy.

Now, if those philosophers, who had nothing to lose by
explaining metaphysical themes were in the habit of using allusions and figurative language when discussing them, surely
we, observant Jews, should not explain to the general public
a subject too hard for them to understand, for it might be
taken as the opposite of the true meaning. Bear this in mind.

CHAPTER 18

——◄◉►——

The Meaning of קרב—*Come Near,*
נגש—*Approach* and נגע—*Touch*

The three words: קרב, *to come near,* נגש, *to approach,* and
נגע, *to touch,* denote *contact* or *nearness in space.*
Sometimes they mean, *to come to understand something.* קרב
is used in the sense of *to come near a certain spot* in, *As
[Moshe] neared the camp (Shemos 32:19); "And Pharaoh came
close " (ibid. 14:10).* נגע in the sense of *to touch physically* occurs in, *"And she **touched** it to his feet" (ibid. 4:25); "He
touched it to my mouth" (Yeshayah 6:7).* And נגש in the sense
of *to approach* or *to move toward another person* is found in,
*"Yehudah **approached** up to [Yosef]" (Bereishis 44:18).*

The second meaning of these three words is metaphoric,
to come to understand something or *reaching someone mental-
ly* but not involving space. Regarding נגע—*to touch* in the
metaphoric sense we have the verse, *"For her punishment
touches heaven" (Yirmiyah 51:9).* And for קרב—*come near* in

the metaphoric sense of giving information we have, *"If a case is too difficult, **bring it near** to me" (Devarim 1:17);* in other words, *let me know about it.* The verb *bring it near* is used here in the sense of giving information. The verb נגש— *approach* is used metaphorically in, *"And Avraham came forward and said" (Bereishis 18:23).* [He did not actually step up to Hashem.] This took place in a prophetic vision and a prophetic dream state, as will be explained [in Chapter 21]. We find this figurative meaning used also in the verse, *"Because that people has **approached** Me with its mouth and honored Me with its lips" (Yeshayah 29:13).* Wherever you find in the Prophets that a person approached or came close to Hashem it should be interpreted in a figurative sense, [i.e. to approach mentally]. For Hashem is not corporeal, and consequently, He does not approach or come close to anything. When a Being is not physical it does not occupy space, and the concepts of approach, contact, distance, attachment, separation, touch or closeness do not apply to it.

I don't think that you harbor any doubts about the following verses: *"Hashem is **close** to all who call upon him" (Tehillim 145:18); "They are eager for the **nearness** of God" (Yeshayah 58:2); "As for me, **nearness** to God is good" (Tehillim 73:28).* You understand that all these phrases suggest a spiritual closeness—the attainment of knowledge—not a closeness in space.

HASHEM IS EVERYWHERE

However, if you want to interpret the verse, *"Only Moshe shall **approach** Hashem, the others may not come close" (Shemos 24:2),* to mean that Moshe should approach a place on the mountain where the Divine Light was shining, you may. Just keep in mind that no matter whether a person is standing at the center of the earth or at the highest point of the ninth sphere,[9] if this were possible, he is no further away from Hashem in the one case, or no nearer to Him in the other. Only those who gain knowledge of Him come close to Him, and those who are ignorant of Him move away. There are many degrees by which a person can come closer to God or move away from Him. I will elaborate on this.

CHAPTER 19

---===⬥===---

THE MEANING OF מלא—*TO FILL*

The word מלא, *to fill,* is a word of many meanings. Linguistic scholars define the term as *to put into a container as much of something as it will hold.* For example, "*She filled her pitcher*" (Bereishis 24:16); "*Fill an omer measure [of the manna]*" (Shemos 16:32). There are many other instances. It also denotes the end or termination of a fixed period of time, as in, "*When the time was filled (came) for her to give birth*" (Bereishis 25:24); "*When the forty days were filled (completed)*" (Bereishis 50:3). Next, it signifies reaching the highest degree of perfection, as in, "*Filled with Hashem's blessing*" (Devarim 33:23); "*He has filled them with wisdom of heart*" (Shemos 35:35); "*He was filled with wisdom, understanding and talent*" (1 Melachim 7:14). In this sense it says, "*The whole earth is full of His glory*" (Yeshayah 6:4), which means "*The whole earth is proof of His perfection.*" Similarly, "*The*

---

9. Ancient astronomers believed that there were nine concentric transparent globes, called spheres, revolving around the earth, carrying the various heavenly bodies.

glory of Hashem filled the Tabernacle" (Shemos 40:34) [mean-
ing, God's presence was evident in the Tabernacle]. In fact,
wherever the verb *to fill* occurs with reference to Hashem it
must be interpreted this way. God is not a body that takes up
space. However, in this situation if you think that the phrase
the glory of Hashem refers to a special light created for this
purpose, and it filled the Tabernacle, I see nothing wrong.

CHAPTER 20

THE MEANING OF רם—*ELEVATED*, AND נשא—*LIFTED*

The word נשא is defined as *elevation* either in space or in
importance, i.e. in greatness, honor and glory. Elevation
in the sense of space occurs in, *"[The ark] rose from the
ground" (Bereishis 7:17)*; and in the sense of elevation in importance in, *"I have raised (exalted) the one chosen from
among the people" (Tehillim 89:20); "I raised you up from
among the people" (1 Melachim 14:7)*.

Whenever this word is used in reference to Hashem, it is
in the second sense, for example, *"Be elevated (exalted) above
the heavens, O God" (Tehillim 57:12)*.

THE MEANING OF נשא—TO LIFT

In the same way, the verb נשא *to lift up* denotes both elevation in space and elevation in status and importance, [but
נשא—*lift* indicates a higher degree of elevation than רם—

elevate.] An example of *lift* in the sense of elevation in space is, *"They **lifted** (loaded) the food they bought on their donkeys" (Bereishis 42:26).* There are many instances like this where the verb *lift* means *to carry,* for this implies elevation in space. In the second sense [of elevation in status] there are the verses, *"His kingdom shall be **lifted** (exalted)" (Bamidbar 24:7); "He raised them and **lifted** (exalted) them" (Yeshayah 63:9); "Why are you **lifting** (setting) yourselves (above) God's congregation?" (Bamidbar 16:3).*

Whenever this verb occurs in any of its forms with reference to the Creator it is meant in the metaphoric sense, for example, *"**Lift** Yourself up, O judge of the earth" (Tehillim 94:2); "For thus said He Who is high and **lifted** (exalted)" (Yeshayah 57:15),* where *lifted* signifies elevation in status, importance and authority, not elevation in space.

You may find it difficult to understand that I lump together the terms *status, importance* and *authority,* and you may ask, "How can you say that several different expressions denote the same thing?" You will find out later that accomplished thinkers do not consider Hashem Yisbarach as having many different attributes, rather the numerous attributes that describe His Might, Greatness, Power, Perfection, Goodness etc. are all identical. They are terms referring to His Essence and not to anything other than His Essence.

In future chapters I will deal with the Names and Attributes of God. For now I only want to show that *high* and *exalted* in the verses I quoted denote elevation in status, not in space.

CHAPTER 21

———◆◆◆———

THE MEANING OF עבר—*TO PASS*

T he primary meaning of the Hebrew verb עבר *to pass* is *to move something from one place to another*. It mainly applies to living creatures moving over some distance in a straight line, as in, *"[Yaakov] passed ahead of them" (Bereishis 33:3); "Pass before the people" (Shemos 17:5)*. Many other examples can be mentioned. Later the meaning of *to pass* was expanded to denote the passage of sound through the air, as in, *"They passed an announcement throughout the camp" (Shemos 36:6);* and, *"The report I hear the people of Hashem passing (spreading) about" (1 Shmuel 2:24)*.

In a figurative sense *to pass* is used to describe the manifestation of the Light and the *Shechinah* that the prophets saw in their prophetic visions, as in, *"A smoking furnace and a flaming torch passed between the halves of the animals" (Bereishis 15:17)*. This took place in a prophetic vision, for the story begins, *"Avram fell into a trance" (ibid. 15:12)*. The verb *to pass* is used in the same metaphoric sense in, *"I will pass through the land of Egypt" (ibid. 12:12)* [meaning, *I will reveal Myself*], and in all similar passages.

Pass is also applied to anyone [or anything] that has gone too far and overstepped his boundaries, as in, *"I have become like one who has passed [the proper limit of] wine to drink" (Yirmiyah 23:9)*.

Furthermore, it is used figuratively to describe a person who missed one target, and turns to a different one, or substitutes a different one for it, as in, *"He shot the arrow, making it pass (miss) the target" (1 Shmuel 20:36)*. I think that *to pass* is used in this sense in, *"Hashem passed by His face"* (Shemos 34:6). I take *His face*[10] to mean *the face of Hashem.* Our Sages also interpreted *his face* as referring to Hashem's face. And although this interpretation is found in the Aggadic section of the Gemara, and does not belong in this work, it lends support to our view that *his face* means *Hashem's Face.* It seems that the verse wants to make the following point: Moshe sought to attain a level of understanding that is called *perceiving the Divine face* [the Divine Essence]. But Hashem told him, *"My face [i.e. My Essence] will not be seen" (Shemos 33:23).* However, Hashem promised him a perception of lower degree, this is called, *seeing the Back,* as it says, *"You will see My Back" (ibid.).* [Thus *and He passed* in this verse means Hashem substituted a perception of lower degree for the higher perception Moshe had asked for.]

We discussed this issue in Mishneh Torah *(Yesodei Hatorah 1:10).*

It says here that Hashem withheld from Moshe the kind of perception that is called *seeing the Divine face* [i.e. the knowledge of the Divine Essence], but He gave him instead another gift: the knowledge of the acts attributed to Hashem, as I will explain [in Chapter 24]. When I say Hashem withheld from Moshe the higher perception, I do not mean to say Hashem denied Moshe his request, but that this knowledge is beyond human reach, and by its very nature unattainable to Moshe. A person can gain perfection as long as he applies his mind to things within the reach of his intellect, but if he seeks a higher degree of understanding he will lose his mind or die—as I will explain [in Chapters 31-34]—unless Hashem grants him His help, as Hashem said to Moshe, *"I*

---

10. Simply understood this verse means that Hashem passed before Moshe's face. The Rambam explained it to mean that Hashem passed by or substituted something in place of His face.

will place My hand over you [meaning, protecting you with My power], until I pass by" (Shemos 33:22).

THE APPROACH OF TARGUM ONKELOS

Targum Onkelos, in translating this verse, follows the approach he uses in explaining similar passages: Whenever there is an expression describing Hashem in corporeal terms or ascribing physical attributes to Him, the Targum assumes a word is missing, and inserts that word before Hashem's Name. In the verse, *"And Hashem was standing over him"* *(Bereishis 28:13),* [which ascribes corporeality to Hashem], he translates, *"The glory of Hashem was standing over him."* In the verse, *"Hashem will keep watch between me and you"* *(Bereishis 31:49),* he paraphrases, *The word of Hashem will keep watch.* This he does throughout his translation. *"Hashem passed by before his face"* *(Shemos 34:6),* he renders, *"Hashem caused His Shechinah to pass before his face and called."* According to this translation, what passed was undoubtedly a physical object, and the pronoun *his* [in *his face,*]refers to Moshe. The interpretation of Targum Onkelos is also fitting and correct.

You should not be surprised that a subject as profound and complex as this can be interpreted in different ways. This does not weaken the point we made. You may choose the opinion you prefer. You may consider the entire episode as a prophetic vision, regarding the thing that Moshe wanted, and was withheld from him, and what he received instead, as something that was perceived only by the intellect. Or you may assume that, in addition, there was a certain visual perception of a material object, which helped the prophet to attain intellectual perception.

You may also say that there was a perception of sound, and

a voice passed before him which was something physical. You may choose any of these opinions, our only purpose is to guard against interpreting the phrase, *Hashem passed,* like *"pass before the people" (Shemos 17:5)* [which is used in a physical sense]. Since Hashem is not a physical body, you cannot say He moves, therefore the verb *to pass* in its primary meaning cannot apply to Him.

CHAPTER 22

The Meaning of בא—*To Come*

The Hebrew verb בא means *to come* as it relates to a living being. It denotes a person's arrival at a place or his approach to a person, as in, *"Your brother came with deceit" (Bereishis 27:35).* It also signifies *to enter* a place, as in, *"When Yosef entered the house" (ibid. 43:26); "When you enter the land" (Shemos 12:25).* The verb is used in a figurative sense to denote the coming of an event, that is, [the arrival of] something intangible, as in, *"We should like to honor you when your words come true" (Shofetim 13:17); "Whatever will come upon you" (Yeshayah 47:13);* yes, *come* can even refer to the arrival of ruin, as in *"And trouble came" (Iyov 3:26).* Since the word *come* has been used for intangible things, it has also been applied to Hashem—to express the fulfillment of His word or to the appearance of His *Shechinah.* It is in this sense that we must understand the verses, *"I will come to you in a thick cloud" (Shemos 19:9),* and, *"Hashem, the God of Israel has entered through [this gate]" (Yechezkel 44:2).* In these and all similar verses the manifestation of the *Shechinah* is meant. But when it says, *"And Hashem my God will come"* (*Zechariah 14:5*), the meaning is *His word will come,* in other words, the promises He made through His prophets will be fulfilled. That's why the passage ends, *"all the holy ones that are with you,"* that is to say, *The word of Hashem my God will come true, that has been prophesied by all the holy men who are with you, who speak to Israel.*

CHAPTER 23

THE MEANING OF יצא—*TO GO OUT* AND שוב—*TO RETURN*

The term יצא *to go out* is the opposite of בא *to come in.* יצא *to go out* applies to the movement of a body from where it had been resting to another place, whether the body is a living being or not. For example, *"They had just gone out of the city"* (*Bereishis 44:4*); *"If a fire goes (breaks) out"* (*Shemos 22:5*). It is used in a metaphoric sense to denote the emergence of something intangible, as in, *"No sooner did these words leave the king's lips"* (*Esther 7:8*); *"When what the queen did will go out into the open"* (*Ibid. 1:17*); *"For from Zion will the Torah go forth"* (*Yeshayah 2:3*); and also, *"The sun has gone out (emerged) on the earth"* (*Bereishis 19:23*), meaning, it began to shine.

In this figurative sense we must take every form of, *going out* when it relates to Hashem For example, *"For lo! Hashem shall go out from His place"* (*Yeshayah 26:21*), which means,

The word of Hashem, which has been hidden will go out and will become manifest, in other words, something that has not existed before will come into being; for everything new stemming from Hashem is attributed to His word. For example, *"By the word of Hashem the heavens were made, and by the breath of His mouth all their hosts" (Tehillim 33:6).* This is a figure of speech taken from the way kings act, they use their word as a means of implementing their will. Hashem, however, does not need an instrument to do anything; His works come into being by His will alone. He does not use any kind of speech, as will be explained later.

THE MEANING OF שוב—*RETURN*

The verb יצא, *to go out,* has been used in a figurative sense to describe the emergence of the work of Hashem, as we noted above in our explanation of the verse, *"For Lo, Hashem shall go forth from His place," (Yeshayah 26:21)* [which means that something new will come into being]. In a similar way the verb שוב, *to return,* has been used figuratively to denote the cessation of a certain action by the will of Hashem, as in, *"I will return to My place" (Hoshea 5:15).* This means that the *Shechinah* which has been in our midst has departed from us, and as a result the Divine providence [and protection] over us has been taken away. And so it says in the prophecy of future calamities, *"I will hide My face from them [taking away My providence and Divine protection], and they will be [their enemies'] prey" (Devarim 31:17).* For when Divine protection is taken away, man is open to all dangers, his life will depend on the ups and downs of chance and his fortune and misfortune are a toss-up. What a terrible fate! This is the meaning of *"I will return to My place" (Hoshea 5:15).*

CHAPTER 24

————◆◆◆————

THE MEANING OF הלך—*TO WALK OR GO*

The verb הלך, *to walk-to go*, is a word that denotes motion by living beings, as in, *"And Yaakov **walked** (went) on his way"* (Bereishis 32:2). There are many other examples of this. The meaning was then broadened to apply to objects that are not solid, as in, *"The waters **went** on diminishing"* (Bereishis 8:5); *"And the fire **went** down continuously unto the earth"* (Shemos 9:23). Then it was used figuratively to express the spreading and manifestation of something intangible, as in, *"Its voice shall **go** like a snake"* (Yirmiyah 46:22); and, *"They heard God's voice **moving** about in the garden"* (Bereishis 3:8). It was the voice that was moving, not Hashem.

Whenever the word *went*, or *to go*, is used in connection with Hashem it must be understood in the figurative sense to denote either the manifestation of something incorporeal or the withdrawal of Divine providence. In the Torah this removal of the Divine providence and protection is called *the hiding of God's face*, as in, *"I will utterly hide My face"* (Devarim 31:18). It has also been called *going away* or *moving away from something*, as in, *"I will go and return to My place"* (Hosea 5:15). But in the verse, *"Hashem displayed anger against [Aharon and Miriam], and He **went**"* (Bamidbar 12:9), the two [figurative] meanings of the verb הלך coincide, namely, the withdrawal of the Divine protection, expressed by, *and He went [away]*, and the appearance of something[11], namely, the anger that went forth at them.

---

11. In this context *"and He went"* does not mean and He went away, rather He went and caused Miriam to be punished.

Because of this anger Miriam became leprous, white as snow. The term *to go,* or *to walk* was also applied to indicate how a person should conduct his life. This is an abstract concept having nothing to do with ["walking" or] moving the body, as in, *"Walk in His ways" (Devarim 28:9); "Walk after Hashem your God" (ibid. 13:5); "Come, let us walk by the light of Hashem" (Yeshayah 2:5).*

CHAPTER 25

———◦◉◦———

THE MEANING OF שכן—*TO DWELL*

It is common knowledge that the meaning of שכן is *to dwell* or *live,* as in, *"[Avraham] was living in the plains of Mamrei" (Bereishis 14:13); "And it happened while Yaakov was living undisturbed in the area" (ibid. 35:22).* This is how the word is used in ordinary speech. Dwelling or living in a place implies a long-term stay in that place. When a person stays in a place for a long time we say he lives there, although undoubtedly he moves around, as in *"[Avraham] was living in the plains of Mamrei" (Bereishis 14:13)* and, *"It happened while Yaakov was living undisturbed in the area" (ibid. 35:22).*

The verb *to dwell,* was next applied metaphorically to inanimate objects that rest on something else, although the object is not a living being and the thing on which it rests is not a place. For example, *"May a cloud dwell over [the day]" (Iyov 3:5);* of course, a cloud is not a living being, and a day is not a tangible thing, but a portion of time.

In this sense the word *dwell* is used with reference to Hashem, to denote the endlessness of His *Shechinah* or His providence in a place, or to signify an object where *Shechinah* is present constantly. For example, *"Hashem's glory **dwelled** (rested) on Mount Sinai" (Shemos 24:16); "I will **dwell** among B'nei Yisrael" (ibid. 29:45),* [meaning, *"I will make My presence felt"*]; *"And the favor of the One Who **dwells** in the thorn-bush" (Devarim 33:16).*

Whenever the term *dwell* is applied to Hashem, it must be taken to mean either "the continuous presence of His *Shechinah,"* i.e. His Light that is manifest in that place, or *His Providence and Supervision protecting a certain object,* [depending on the context].

CHAPTER 26

---◆◉◆---

THE TORAH SPEAKS THE ORDINARY LANGUAGE OF MEN

You surely are familiar with the Talmudic rule underlying the interpretations of the previous chapters. I mean the rule: דברה תורה כלשון בני אדם, *The Torah speaks the ordinary language of men,* that is to say, the Torah describes the Creator in terms easily understood by everyone. Hashem is depicted as having attributes that imply corporeality in order to express His existence; because common people cannot easily comprehend existence unless it is tangible; something that is bodiless has no meaning to them. In addition, whatever we consider perfection is attributed to Hashem to express that He is perfect in every respect, and no imperfection or flaw is found in Him. Anything that people generally consider a defect or imperfection is not attributed to Hashem; that's why He is never portrayed as eating, drinking,[12] sleeping, being sick or violent, or anything like that. On the other hand, whatever the public mind views as perfection—albeit only human perfection, [which in relation to Hashem is actually the height of imperfection]—is attributed to Him.

WHY MOTION IS APPLIED TO HASHEM

You know, that motion is one of the distinguishing characteristics of living beings, a person cannot exist without motion if he wants to achieve perfection. Just as a person has to eat, drink and excrete waste, so must he move to get things that are good and pleasant for him and to avoid things that are harmful and unpleasant. It should make no difference whether we ascribe to Hashem eating, drinking or motion; but in the common perception, eating and drinking are thought of as imperfections and motion is not, although you move because you need something, [making motion as much an imperfection as eating and drinking].

It has been proven that everything that moves is tangible and separable. We know that Hashem is not physical and the concepts of motion and rest do not apply to Him; rest can only be applied to something that also moves. Thus when we say Hashem *moves* or *lives,* it must be understood in a figurative sense. For *motion* and *life* are concepts that apply only to living beings. You could never use any of the following

---

12. Eating and drinking are considered imperfections.A person eats because he is hungry and needs food. He lacks something, thus he is imperfect.

expressions: to go down, to go up, to walk, to stand, to sur-
round, to sit, to dwell, to go out, to come in, to pass, and the
like, in reference to something intangible.

The reason we elaborated more than usual on this subject
is because people are used to the notion, [of attributing corporeality to God]. It is necessary to clarify this subject, as we
have done, for the benefit of those who strive to acquire perfection, to eliminate misconceptions that have been ingrained in their minds since childhood.

CHAPTER 27

AN UNUSUAL TRANSLATION BY TARGUM ONKELOS

Onkelos the Convert who was thoroughly familiar with the
Hebrew and the Aramaic languages made it his goal to eliminate the [erroneous] belief in God's corporeality. So, wherever he found an expression in the Torah that tended to ascribe corporeality to Hashem he paraphrased it consistent
with the context. All expressions having to do with motion
he renders as the appearance or manifestation of a certain
light, i.e. the *Shechinah* or *Hashgachah* (Divine Supervision,
Providence). He translates, *"Hashem will come down"*
(Shemos 19:11) as *"Hashem will manifest Himself."* The
phrase *"I will go down and see" (Bereishis 18:21)* he renders,
"I will manifest Myself and see." This is the way [he translates
the verb ירד, *to go down,*] throughout his work [whenever it
is used with reference to Hashem.] The only exception is the
following, *"[Hashem said to Yaakov,] 'I will go down to Egypt*

with you'" (*Bereishis 46:4*) which he translates literally, [and is not concerned about the corporeality implied by *going down.*] This an extraordinary proof of this great man's genius, the excellence of his commentary and the accuracy of his interpretation. For through his translation he is teaching us an important principle regarding prophecy:

The story opens: *"And Elohim (God) spoke to Israel in a night vision, and said, 'Yaakov! Yaakov!' . . . 'I will go down to Egypt with you.'"* (*Bereishis 2,4*). Since this episode is introduced as a vision of the night [i.e a dreamlike trance rather than a lucid prophecy], Onkelos did not hesitate to translate literally the words said to Yaakov in his nighttime vision. The verse relates what Yaakov was told, not what actually took place. Unlike the passage, *"And Hashem came down on Mount Sinai"* (*Shemos 19:20*), which is an account of what actually occurred in the physical world, in which Onkelos paraphrases *Hashem came down* as, *Hashem manifested Himself,* to avoid the idea of motion [that is implied by *Hashem came down.*] By contrast, when translating things told to a person [in a prophetic dream] Onkelos leaves the quote unchanged. Truly amazing!

From the above you may draw the conclusion that there is a great difference in Divine messages. There is a message that is conveyed in a dream, another that is given in a vision, some simply start with the words, *"And the word of Hashem came to me, saying,"* or *"Hashem said to me."*

In my opinion, it could be that Onkelos understood the word *Elohim* in the above mentioned passage *["And Elohim said to Israel"]* to represent an *angel,* [as explained in Chapter two that the word Elohim sometimes refers to an angel,] that is the reason why he had no objection to translate literally, *"I will go down to Egypt with you."*[13] I don't think

---

13. Because an angel could have indeed gone down with him to Egypt.

it is farfetched to say that Onkelos should believe the one who said to Yaakov, *"I am the God of your father,"* was an angel, for this could very well have been said by an angel. After all, Yaakov said [earlier], *"And the angel of God said to me in a dream, 'Yaakov' and I replied, 'Yes.'"* (*Bereishis 31:11*). Yaakov concludes the report of the angel's words to him in the following way: *"[The angel said:] I am the God of Bethel, where you anointed a pillar and made an oath to Me"* (*ibid. 13*), there is no doubt that Yaakov made a vow to God and not to the angel. It is the standard way of the prophets to relate words that were spoken to them by an angel in the name of God, as if God himself had spoken to them. Consequently, these verses should be understood as though the angel was saying, *"I am the messenger of the God of your father,"* *"I am the messenger of God Who appeared to you in Bethel,"* and the like.

The various levels of prophecy and the nature of angels will be discussed in future chapters.

CHAPTER 28

THE MEANING OF רגל—FOOT

The word רגל—*foot* is a term of many meanings. First of all it denotes the foot of a living creature, as in, *"A foot for a foot"* (*Shemos 21:24*). Next it signifies an object that follows another, as in, *"Leave! You and all the people that **are at your feet** (your followers),"* (*Shemos 11:8*).

Sometimes *foot* means *cause* [or *because*], because

something done at ones feet connotes something done in ones presence meaning he is the cause of it. There are many examples of this, as in, *"Hashem blessed you **at my feet** (because of me)"* *(Bereishis 30:30)*, i.e. on account of me, and *"**At the feet of** (because of) the cattle that goes before me and because of the children"* *(ibid. 33:14)*. Taken in this sense, the words *his feet* in the verse, *"On that day, **His feet** will stand on the Mount of Olives,"* *(Zechariah 14:4)* refers to the things He caused and brought about, and the meaning of the verse is, *"The wonders that will then be seen on that place, that Hashem **caused** to be, will endure."* Yonasan ben Uziel seems to follow this interpretation, for he renders this passage, *"And He will appear in His might on that day on the Mount of Olives."* As a rule he translates as *Hashem's might* any actions [by Hashem] that involve touching or movement, because all such expressions describe acts done by His Will.

THE THRONE OF GLORY

As you know, in the passage, [whose literal meaning is,] *"And under **His feet** was something like the works of the whiteness of sapphire stone"* *(Shemos 24:10)*, Onkelos, takes *His feet* as an allegorical representation of the Throne, and interprets the words *and under His feet* as *and under the Throne of His Glory*. When you think about it, you will admire how careful Onkelos is to avoid any semblance of corporeality and anything that remotely could give rise to it. He does not say, *and under His Throne*, for if he would relate the Throne to God, the implication would be that God is supported by a material object, which suggests the corporeality of God. Instead, he connects the Throne to Hashem's Glory, i.e. the *Shechinah* which is a [spiritual] light.

Similarly, Targum Onkelos paraphrases the words, *"The*

Hand is on God's Throne" (Shemos 17:16) as, *"An oath has been made by God, Whose Shechinah is on the Throne of His Glory."* We digressed from the subject of this chapter and touched on things that will be dealt with in other chapters; we will now return to the theme at hand.

We made you familiar with the interpretation by Onkelos [of, *"And under His feet was something like the action of the whiteness of a sapphire stone"* to mean *"Under the Throne of His Glory"*]. His main concern is to eliminate from his translation any hint of corporeality in reference to Hashem, but he does not explain [the end of the verse which describes what the elders of Israel] actually perceived, or the meaning of the symbolic images they saw.

THE EXPLANATION OF THE VISION OF WHITE SAPPHIRE

But, in keeping with the purpose of this book, we feel duty-bound to offer an explanation. Our opinion is that the phrase *under His feet* means *that which became because of His presence—that which exists because of Him*—as we explained above. Thus the elders of Israel saw the primordial substance of Creation which emanated from Him and which He brought into being. Now consider the end of the verse, *"like the works of the whiteness of sapphire stone."* If the verse wanted to tell us the color[14] of the stone it would have said, *"like the whiteness of sapphire stone."* But the word *works* or *actions* was added, because, as you know, matter is always inactive

---

14. The simple translation of this verse would seem to be that *Beneath His feet they saw the **appearance** of white sapphire.* The Rambam points out that the word כמעשה is not the usual word for appearance and should be translated as *the workings*; the word *white*-the Rambam explains to mean the transparency of sapphire. The meaning according to this is, *and caused by His presence was like the workings of transparent sapphire.* Meaning; they perceived how the source and fundamental particles of all matter emanate from Him.

and it is active only in rare instances. On the other hand, form, in and of itself, is always active, and only inactive in certain cases, as is explained in books of physics. That's why the phrase *like the workings* has been added in connection with the primordial substance of Creation.

The phrase, *the whiteness of sapphire stone* refers to transparency, not to the color white; for *the whiteness* of the sapphire does not mean white but the characteristic of being transparent. Things that are transparent have no color, as it is explained in books on physics. For if they had a color they would not allow all the colors to pass through them. Only when a transparent object is totally colorless does it permit all colors to pass through. In this respect [the transparency of the sapphire] is like the primordial substance of Creation, which was entirely formless, and thus received all forms [like transparent matter that permits all colors to pass through]. Therefore, what the elders of Israel perceived was the primordial matter, the essential substance of Creation, which is the source of all things which exist and are subject to change. We will discuss this more in later chapters.

Notice that you still need an explanation like the above, even when you accept Onkelos' interpretation of the beginning of the verse as *and under the Throne of His Glory*[15]. The principal aim of every thinking person should be to banish from his mind the thought of attributing corporeality to Hashem, and to believe that all those perceptions [of the elders of Israel] were of a spiritual and not of a material nature. Consider it and bear it in mind.

---

15. Although the Rambam and Onkelos differ as to the interpretation of *under His feet* at the beginning of the verse, the Rambam points outs that *the workings of the whiteness of sapphire* at the end of the verse must be explained as referring to primordial matter even according to Onkelos.

CHAPTER 29

———◦◉◦———

The Meaning of עצב—*Pain*

The word עצב *pain* has several meanings. First, it signifies pain and trembling, as in, *"It will be with **pain** that you will give birth to children"* (Bereishis 3:16). It also denotes anger, as in, *"His father had never **pained him** (made him angry)"* (I Melachim 1:6); *"For he was **pained** (angry) because of David"* (1 Shmuel 20:34). עצב—*Pain* can also stand for rebelliousness, as in *"But they **pained** (rebelled) and grieved His holy spirit"* (Yeshayah 63:10); *"They **pained** (rebelled) against Him in the desert"* (Tehillim 78:40); *"And see if I have **vexing** ways"* (ibid. 139:24); *"Every day they **rebel** against My ways"* (ibid. 56:6).

The passage, *"[Hashem] was **pained** in His heart"* (Bereishis 6:6) can be interpreted both according to the second or third meaning of the word *pain*, [the second *anger*, the third, *rebellion*]. If we take *pain* to denote anger, the phrase *"[Hashem] was **pained** in His heart"* means that Hashem was angry with them because of the wickedness of their deeds. Listen to my explanation of the expression *in His heart* used here and in the story of Noach (ibid. 8:21).

When we speak of a person we use the expression, *he said to himself* or *he said in his heart* to indicate he was thinking about something but did not tell anyone. Similarly, the phrase *Hashem said in His heart* is used with regard to something Hashem wanted to happen but did not mention to a prophet. To ascribe a human characteristic to Hashem is permissible since "The Torah speaks in the ordinary language of men." This is plain and simple. The Torah does not mention that the wicked generation of the Flood received a message warning them of their impending death, that is why it says, Hashem was angry with them *in His heart*. The same way, when Hashem decided there should never again be a flood, He did not tell a prophet to proclaim it to mankind. That's why it says, *"Hashem said in his heart" (Bereishis 8:21)*.

If we take *pain* in the third meaning [*to be rebellious*], we interpret *"And he was pained in His heart"* not to mean, *He (Hashem) was pained in His heart,* but *And he (man) pained His (Hashem's) heart,* meaning *And man rebelled against God's will,* because *heart* also denotes *will*, as we will explain [in Chapter 39] in our discussion of the various meanings of *heart*.

CHAPTER 30

THE MEANING OF אכל—*TO EAT*

The primary definition of אכל—*to eat* is to take in food; this needs no illustration. As the language developed, the concept of eating was broadened to include two aspects; (1) the consumption of the food, [after it is eaten], meaning the destruction of its original form; (2) the growth of living creatures, the maintenance of their health and existence, and the promotion of physical and intellectual strength through food intake.

The verb *to eat* in the first of the two aspects [that of loss and destruction] came to be used figuratively in the sense of *consuming, destroying,* and stripping away the form of something, as in, *"The land of your enemies will **devour** you"* (*Vayikra 26:38*); *"A land that **devours** its inhabitants"* (*Bamidbar 13:32*); *"You will be **devoured** by the sword"* (*Yeshayah 1:20*); *"Shall the sword **devour** forever?"* (*2 Shmuel 2:26*); *"God's fire flared out **consuming** the edge of the camp"* (*Bamidbar 11:1*); *"Hashem your God is like a **consuming** fire"* (*Devarim 4:24*), meaning, He destroys those who rebel against Him, just like fire destroys everything it touches. There are many other examples of this.

With reference to the second aspect of eating, [that of *growth, health* and *intelligence*] the verb *to eat* is figuratively used in the sense of *gaining wisdom* and *learning* for learning nurtures the human intellect just as food nurtures the body. For example, *"Come, buy food and eat"* (*Yeshayah 55:1*) [i.e. an invitation to come and learn Torah]; *"Give heed to Me, and you shall eat choice food"* (*ibid. 2*); *"It is not good to eat much honey"* (*Mishlei 25:27*); *"My son, eat honey for it is good; let its sweet drops be on your palate. Know: such is wisdom for your soul"* (*ibid. 24:13,14*).

The Sages of the Talmud too, often use the verb *to eat* metaphorically in the sense of gaining wisdom, like for example, *Why don't you eat fat meat at the yeshivah of Rava [where the teaching is so much better]?* (*Bava Basra 22a*); *All expressions of eating and drinking that occur in the book of Mishlei refer to wisdom,* (*Koheles Rabbah 3:13*) or according to another version, *All drinking that occur in the Torah refer to wisdom.* Wisdom has also frequently been called *water,* for example, *"Ho, all who are thirsty, come for water!"* (*Yeshayah 55:1*).

The metaphoric meaning of these expressions has become so widely used that people began to think that this was its primary meaning, and the terms *hunger* and *thirst* were used in the sense of *lack of wisdom and intelligence,* as in, *"I will send a famine upon the land: not a hunger for bread or a thirst for water, but for hearing the words of Hashem"* (*Amos 8:11*);

"My soul thirsts for God, the living God" *(Tehillim 42:3).*
There are many examples of this. The passage, *"Joyfully shall
you draw water from the fountains of salvation"* *(Yeshayah
12:3)* is paraphrased by Yonasan ben Uziel as follows: *"You
will joyfully receive new teaching from the chosen of the righteous."* Notice how he explains *water* to symbolize the wisdom that will be attained in those days, and how he interprets *the fountains* as if it were the same as *the leaders* or *the
wise.* By his translation [of the phrase *from the fountains of
salvation* as] *from the chosen of the righteous* he implies that
righteousness is the genuine salvation. So you see how he ex-
pounds every word in this verse as referring to wisdom and
learning. Reflect on this.

CHAPTER 31

———◉———

THE LIMITS OF THE HUMAN INTELLECT

You should be aware that there are concepts and ideas that
are within the reach of the human mind, and on the
other hand, there exist things that the mind cannot grasp;
and no matter how hard a person tries, the gates of perception are closed to him. Then again, there are things that the
mind can understand up to a point, but he remains ignorant
of the rest. Even though a person is able to understand certain things, that does not mean that he must be able to comprehend everything. A fitting analogy is our senses: Our
senses can perceive things up to a point, but not at every
distance. All powers of the body are equally limited. For

example, a man can carry two *kikkar*, but he cannot carry ten *kikkar*. Everyone knows that some individuals of the same species have sharper senses and greater physical prowess than others, but there is a limit to their superiority, their power does not extend to every distance or every dimension.

It is exactly the same when it comes to the human intellect. There is a great difference between one person and another with regard to intellectual faculties, as is well known to philosophers. While one person can discover something by himself, another person will never be able to understand it. Even if he was taught over a long period of time, [by instructors] using the best teaching methods and all possible analogies, his mind simply cannot grasp it, his brain does not have the capacity to absorb it. But the superior mind is not unlimited. A boundary is undoubtedly set for the human intellect beyond which it cannot reach. There are things [beyond that boundary] that are closed to human understanding, you don't even desire to comprehend them, since you know there is no way to attain this knowledge. For example, we don't know the number of stars, whether the number is even or odd; we don't know the number of animals, minerals, or plants, and the like. There are other things which man feels he does have the capacity to understand and very much wants to know; tremendous efforts to explore and investigate these things have been made by thinkers of all nations, at all times. They have different opinions and disagree, they constantly raise new doubts, because they are filled with an insatiable desire to understand these things. Each one believes that he has discovered the right approach to the true knowledge of the thing, although the human mind is unable to offer proof to settle the matter. For a theory that can be substantiated by convincing evidence is not subject to dispute, denial or rejection. Only a fool would contradict it, and a contradiction like that is called, "denial of a proven fact;" just as you may find people who deny that the earth is round or that the orbits of the stars are circular, and the like. Such people cannot begin to understand the subjects that are discussed in the present work.

We find this confusion mostly in metaphysical subjects, somewhat less in questions relating to physics, and there are no disputes at all when it comes to the exact sciences. Alexander Hapardusi said that there are three things that keep people from arriving at the exact truth: first, arrogance and aggressiveness; second, the subtlety, depth, and difficulty of the subject being studied; and third, ignorance and the inability to understand things that can be comprehended. Those are the reasons listed by Alexander. Today we have a fourth reason—one he did not mention because it did not exist in his days—namely, habit and training. It is human nature for people to like and to prefer things they are accustomed to. You can see how true this is by looking at peasants. Although they rarely take a bath, have few enjoyments and live from hand to mouth, they dislike city life and are not attracted to its pleasures, preferring the mediocre things they are accustomed to rather than the good things found in cities. They would not relish living in a mansion, dressing in silks, or indulging in baths, ointments and perfumes.

PRECONCEIVED IDEAS ABOUT HASHEM

The same can be said about opinions a person harbored all his life: he is comfortable with them, defends them, and rejects new ideas. This [familiarity with stale ideas] is another thing that prevents people from finding the truth, and makes them stick to the opinions they are used to. This is the case with the commonly held misconception about the corporeality of Hashem and other metaphysical issues, as we will explain. It stems from long familiarity with verses of Tanach whose plain meaning implies the corporeality of God and other false ideas. The truth is, that these passages were meant to be taken as figures of speech and metaphors. The reason why the Torah used such imagery will be explained later.

Do not think what we have said about the inadequacy of our understanding and its limitations is based only on the Torah, [where it says *"A man cannot have a vision of Me." "My essence itself, will not be seen" (Shemos 33:20,23)*], for philosophers say the same thing. They understand it perfectly, independent of any religion or opinion. It is a fact which is doubted only by people who question things that have been fully proven. This chapter is meant to be an introduction to the next.

CHAPTER 32

MORE ON THE LIMITS OF THE HUMAN INTELLECT

When you read this book, be aware that the thinking process, since it is connected with your brain which is matter, is governed by the same conditions that regulate physical perception [i.e. seeing and hearing]. To put it simply: When you look with your eyes you can see all that your eyes are capable of perceiving, [but you cannot see microscopically small objects or distant galaxies]. However, if you overstrain your eyes and try to focus on an object that is too far away, or to decipher writings or engravings that are too small for your eyesight, forcing yourself to get a clear view, you will dim

your view not only of the object you are straining to see, but
even of things you normally can see clearly. Your eyes will
have become too weak to see things you were able to see before you tried too hard and overreached the limits of your
vision.

The same is true when it comes to the mental processes of
a person who studies science. If a person studies too hard and
racks his brain he will get confused and will not be able to
understand even the things he usually grasps with ease. For
the [physical and mental] powers of the body are the same in
this regard.

When it comes to abstract thinking the same conditions
apply. If you admit that there are things that are unknowable;
and do not try to prove things that cannot be proven, or try
to reject and disavow a statement that has never been refut-
ed, or attempt to understand things beyond your perception,
then you have attained the pinnacle of human perfection,
you are like Rabbi Akiva who "entered in peace [into the
study of the mystical realm of metaphysics] and came out in
peace" (Chagigah 15b). But if you go beyond the limits of
your intellectual power, and begin to deny things that have
not been proven to be impossible, you will be like Elisha
Acher[16](Chagigah 14b). Not only will you fail to become
perfect, but you will drop to the lowest level of imperfection.
Your thoughts will be dominated by fantasies and will show
a proclivity toward imperfection and a sordid and corrupt
way of life. This happens because of the confusion that will
trouble your mind and the dimness that will obscure its light,
just as weakness of eyesight causes sick people to see many
kinds of bizarre images, especially after they looked intently
at very bright or very small objects.

---

16. Elisha ben Avuyah, a Tanna, was one of the four scholars who *entered the* pardes,
i.e. he studied the mysteries of the higher world. He renounced Judaism and became an apostate.

Concerning the idea [of staying within the limits of your intellect] it says, *"If you find honey, eat only what you need, lest you fill yourself with it, and throw it up" (Mishlei 25:16)*. Our Sages applied this verse to Elisha Acher, and what a fitting analogy it is! In comparing knowledge to food (as we mentioned in chapter 30), [Shlomoh Hamelech, the author of Mishlei] mentions the sweetest food, honey. If you eat too much honey it irritates the stomach and makes you throw up. He is saying, that as great, excellent, and wonderful knowledge may be, it is harmful if you don't keep it within its bounds and guard it carefully. Knowledge is just like honey: if you eat it in moderation it is nutritious and tasty, but if you eat too much it will go to waste. That's why it does not say, *lest you fill yourself with it and loathe it,* but *lest you throw it up,* [meaning, it will go to waste]. The same idea is expressed in the verse, *"It is not good to eat too much honey" (Mishlei 25:27);* and, *"Don't act the wise man to excess, or you may be dumbfounded" (Koheles 7:16); "Guard your foot when you go to the house of God" (ibid. 5:1)*. David had this idea in mind when he said, *"I did not pursue matters too great and too wondrous for me" (Tehillim 131:2)*. Our Sages meant this when they stated, "Do not seek things too hard for you, do not search out things that are hidden from you. Study the things you are allowed to, you have no business delving into mysteries" (Chagigah 13a). They meant to say that you should apply your mind only to things the human intellect can grasp, for the study of things beyond human comprehension is extremely harmful, as we have explained.

It was not the intention of our Prophets and our Sages to close the door on research altogether and to prevent the mind from understanding what is within its reach, as fools and lazy people think. These fools are happy to present their ignorance and stupidity as marks of wisdom and perfection, and consider the erudition and wisdom of others as signs of impiety and desertion of Judaism. They are turning darkness into light and light into darkness. The whole purpose of the Prophets and the Sages [instructions not to delve to deeply] was to tell us there is a limit to human reason, a point where it must come to a halt. Please don't criticize the words I used in this chapter and in others when I compared the mind to the physical senses, for I only tried to give a general idea of the subject under discussion, not to describe the essence of the intellect. This will be taken up in other chapters.

CHAPTER 33

THE DANGERS OF STUDYING
AND TEACHING METAPHYSICS

You should know that it is very dangerous to begin [a youngster's education] by teaching him the philosophy of metaphysics.[17] It is equally dangerous to explain to him the deeper meaning of analogies that occur in prophecies, and interpret the metaphors used in the stories of the Prophets. Instead, you should instruct the young and less intelligent according to their level of understanding. Those that are intelligent and capable of absorbing a higher level of

---

17. Metaphysics is a branch of philosophy. Students of metaphysics are concerned with reality as a whole, the existence of God, who is the first principle and the final cause of all the universe. They inquire into the relationship of the soul, mind and body, and analyze the concepts of knowledge, reason and perception. They ask: what is the cause of all things? what is existence? what is the essential nature of things? They research such principles as substance and form, potential and actual, and many other abstract themes.

learning, i.e. a level based on proof and logical reasoning, should gradually be promoted toward perfection, either by a teacher or by self-instruction. If a youngster starts out by studying metaphysics he will not only be confused in his religious beliefs but will become completely nonreligious. I compare such a person to a baby that is fed wheat bread, meat and wine. Such an infant will surely die, not because such food is inherently unfit for the human body, but because the child is too weak to digest the food and absorb its nutrients. The same holds true for the principles of metaphysics and the knowledge of the Torah. They were presented in analogies and taught by wise men in the most concealed form they could think of, not because they hide some sinister message, or contradict the fundamental principles of the Torah (as fools who consider themselves philosophers think) but because beginners are unable to fathom their true meaning. Only faint indications have been given as to their real meanings to benefit those capable of understanding them. This knowledge was therefore called *secrets of the Torah*, as we will explain further on.

This is the reason why *the Torah speaks the ordinary language of men*, as we have explained, [because its ideas are extremely profound and cannot not be explained in simple terms]. For the Torah is meant to be studied by the young, the women and the general public, and since they are not able to understand the true sense of the words, the Oral Law [i.e. the Mishnah, Gemara and Midrash] conveyed the true intent of the Torah verses. As far as fundamental principles are concerned, [such as the existence of God, Divine providence, reward and punishment, the incorporeality of God, etc.], the Torah only implies their existence but does not explain their true essence. When a person achieves perfection and attains the knowledge of the *secrets of the Torah*, either through the help of a teacher or, step by step, through self-instruction, he will reach a stage where he steadfastly believes in the true principles [of the Jewish faith], because of conclusive proof and convincing arguments. He will then have a clear idea of the true meaning of the similes and metaphors he was familiar with, and he will fully understand their intent. We mentioned a number of times the rule of our Sages, "Do not discuss the mysteries of the Heavenly Chariot [as described in the first chapter of Yechezkel] even with one student, unless he is wise and astute; and then teach him only the headings of the chapters." Therefore, we may introduce a person to this subject only when his intellect has matured, and only if he meets two conditions, first, that he is wise, meaning, he has mastered the preliminary studies, and second, that he is intelligent, sharp-witted, clear-headed, and quick to grasp an idea. That is what the Mishnah meant when it said the student, *should understand of his own knowledge (Chagigah 11b)*.

In the next chapter I will explain the reasons why we should not teach pure metaphysics to the general public or explain to them the true essence of things.

CHAPTER 34

FIVE PRECAUTIONS BEFORE STUDYING METAPHYSICS

There are five reasons why a person should not study metaphysics unprepared, and why metaphysics should not be taught to the general public.

The First Reason: The subject [of metaphysics] itself is

difficult, complex, and profound, *"It is elusive and deep, deep down; who can discover it?" (Koheles 7:24)*. It also says [about metaphysics], *"Whence does wisdom come, where is the source of understanding?" (Iyov 28:20)*. You should not begin studying difficult and esoteric subjects. One of the common metaphors in the Torah, is that wisdom is compared to water. The Sages said: If a person knows how to swim he will bring up pearls from the seabed, but if he cannot swim he will drown. Therefore only an experienced swimmer should jump into the deep waters of metaphysics.

OBSTACLES TO INTELLECTUAL GROWTH

The Second Reason: At the outset, a person's intelligence is inadequate, because in his early years he is not at the peak of perfection. He has only the potential of attaining perfection, but does not actually have it. As it says, *"Man is born a wild ass" (Iyov 11:12)*. Even if a person has the potential [i.e. the aptitude] for a skill, that does not necessarily mean this skill will become a reality. It may be that he never develops it, either because of some obstacle, or because he may lack the training necessary to turn the aptitude into a reality. This thought is expressed in the verse, *"Not many are wise" (Iyov 32:9)*; also our Sages say, "I have seen only few who attained a high degree of perfection" (Sukkah 45b). There are many things that stand in the way of perfection and sidetrack a person from it. He may not find the necessary preparation and time to learn all he needs to know in order to turn his potential perfection into reality.

THE NEED TO STUDY THE SCIENCES

The Third Reason: The mastery of the preliminary studies takes a long time. A person, in his natural desire to reach his goal, often finds these studies too tedious and drops them. You can be sure if a person could reach his aim without preliminary studies, he would cast them aside as a needless bother, [yet these preliminary studies are indispensable]. Suppose you wake someone up—even the most naive person—and tell him: Would you like to know what the heavens are, how many heavens there are, what they look like, and what is inside of them; what are angels; how the world was created; what is its purpose, what is the pattern of everything; what is the soul; how does it enter the body; is there life after death; and if so, how does the soul exist without a body; how does the soul merit afterlife, and what does the soul attach itself to in the afterlife, and similar theoretical questions. That person would surely say, "Yes," and would show a natural curiosity to learn the truth about these things, but he will want to satisfy this curiosity and wish to gain this knowledge only if you summarize it for him in a few words. If you ask him to take off work for a week to learn this, he would not do it. He would be satisfied with imaginary and false ideas and would refuse to believe that these are things needing a great deal of preparation and extensive preliminary research.

FIRST STUDY THE BASIC SCIENCES

But you know that all these subjects are interconnected; for there is nothing else in existence except Hashem and His works, this includes all existing things beside Him. The only way we can obtain knowledge of Him is through His works. His works are proof of His existence, and show what we must believe about Him, in other words, what must be attributed to Him, either in a positive or a negative sense.[18] Therefore it is necessary to examine all things according to their essence, so that by studying every species we arrive at true and accurate conclusions that may help us in finding answers to metaphysical questions. Many mathematical postulates and geometrical figures[19] are helpful in understanding the Divine attributes. You surely don't doubt that the study of astronomy and physics are necessary in order to understand the relationship between the universe and Hashem as it is in reality, and not according to imagined theories.

There are many areas of philosophical inquiry that are unrelated to metaphysics, which, nevertheless are valuable, for they train the mind to think logically and to demand proof to establish the truth. They remove the mix-up from the minds of thinkers who confuse accidental with essential properties,[20] and the wrong opinions that result from such muddled thinking. Therefore, if someone wants to attain human perfection he must first study logic, next the various subdivisions of mathematics, then physics, and only then metaphysics. We find that many people who have progressed a little in the study of these subjects become tired of them and

---

18. Examples of negative Divine attributes: Hashem's existence is not bound by time; He does not have bodily form; nothing resembles Him; He is without beginning; His unity has no end.

19. For example the fact that 1x1=1, shows that the number 1 never changes, something that cannot be said of any other number that is multiplied by itself. Thus you find a reflection of Hashem's unity and permanence in mathematics.Another example is the circle which is one indivisible unbroken line. If it is broken the circle ceases to exist. Thus the circle is a reflection of the idea that Hashem is One, indivisible and unchangeable.

20. Accidental and essential are philosophical terms. To say, for example, of an animal, it is brown, it is large, it is hungry, is to give its *accidental* qualities at the moment. To say of it, it is a horse, is to state the one essential and permanent thing about it, which is its essence. The essence of anything is that in it which gives it continuous and independent existence.

stop; others who don't get bored with the preliminary studies, are forced to interrupt them by death. Now, if we did not
have the Oral Law and oral tradition, and if we were not
given the Biblical metaphors and similes [to tell us what we
must believe], we would have been forced to search by ourselves for the essential truth and to believe only what we
could prove. It would take a long time to accomplish this. If
that were the case, most people would die without ever finding out whether there was a God or not, and they surely
would not know that He had certain positive and negative attributes. From such a fate not even one of a city and two of
a family would escape.

Regarding the survivors, the remnant who invoke the
name of Hashem they only reach the desired perfection after
proper preparation. The necessity of such preparation and
the need for training [in the sciences] before studying metaphysics has been clearly stated by Shlomoh: *"If the ax has become dull, and he has not whetted the edge, he must exert more
strength; and it is advantageous to prepare for wisdom"
(Koheles 10:10); "Listen to advice and accept discipline in
order that you may be wise in the end" (Mishlei 19:20).*

There is still another important reason why the preliminary subjects should be studied and understood. When a student studies hastily and without depth, many doubts crop
up, and he sees very quickly the difficulties and the objec-
tions that are raised against the subject matter, but is unable
to resolve the matter, just as it is easier to tear down a building than to erect it. The only way to substantiate the matter
is to be familiar with the preliminary studies and postulates
taken from them. Whoever studies metaphysics without the
proper preparation is like a person who travels to a place, and
on the road falls into a deep pit from which there is no escape. He will surely perish there. Had he not left home, he
would have been better off.

THERE ARE NO SHORTCUTS TO PERFECTION

Shlomoh has written at great length in Mishlei about lazy people and their sluggishness, which he uses in a figurative sense to describe laziness in the search for wisdom. And so he speaks of a man who eagerly wants to know the final results, but does not make an effort to understand the basic knowledge that leads to it. He only wants to know the bottom line. *"The craving of a lazy man kills him, for his hands refuse to work. All day long he is seized with craving while the righteous man gives without stint"* (Mishlei 21:25,26). He means to say, if the craving kills the lazy man, it is because he does not go after the thing that would satisfy his craving. He does nothing but crave, and hopes to obtain something without using the means to reach it. He would be better off to shake off his craving. Notice how the end of the simile sheds light on its beginning. It concludes with the words, *while the righteous man gives without stint;* to put *righteous* in opposition to *lazy* makes sense only on the basis of our interpretation. Shlomoh is saying that the righteous man gives everything its due share, he spends all the time needed studying the subject and does not devote any time to something else. To put the verse another way: The righteous man devotes his days to wisdom, and does not withhold any of them. The same idea is expressed in the verse, *"Do not give your strength to women"* (Mishlei 31:3), [devote it rather to acquiring wisdom].

Most scholars, that is to say, the most famous scientists, suffer from this disease, rushing to get the final results and speaking about them prematurely. Driven by stupidity or ambition, some scholars disregard the basic studies which they are either unable or too lazy to understand, and try to prove that these basic studies are either harmful or useless. If you give the matter some thought, you will realize the truth [that metaphysics does require a great deal of preparatory study].

METAPHYSICS ONLY FOR THE VIRTUOUS
AND THE MATURE

The Fourth Reason has to do with a person's temperament. It is a proven fact that good character traits are a prerequisite for intellectual excellence. Only a person who is virtuous, calm and serene can be intellectually objective, that is, think straight. Many people have an innate disposition that makes it impossible for them to attain perfection. For example, a person whose heart is by nature hotblooded and who is also very strong cannot help but be wrathful, even if he trained himself to control his fury. Or take a person whose glands are warm, moist and firm, and he produces great quantities of testosterone, he will not be afraid to sin, even if he makes a great effort to restrain himself. Then again there are people who are very loud and boisterous—whose unrepressed and wild gestures prove that they are very sick—in fact, their temperament is so bad that it is incurable. Such persons can never attain perfection, and it is utter folly to try to teach them metaphysics. The science of metaphysics, as you know, is different from the science of medicine and geometry, and not everybody is ready for it, as we mentioned earlier. It is impossible for a person to study it without first acquiring virtuous character traits, the highest degree of integrity and moral perfection, *"For the devious man is an abomination to Hashem, but He is intimate with the straightforward" (Mishlei 3:32).* That's why it is considered inappropriate to teach metaphysics to young men; besides, it is impossible for them to understand it because of their fiery temperament and the youthful ardor that bewilders their minds. That youthful flame which causes all the confusion must first be doused; they must calm down, humble their hearts and become moderate in their personality; only then will they be able to rise to the level of the perception of Hashem, i.e. the study of metaphysics which is called *The Works of the Divine Chariot.* As it says, *"Hashem is close to the brokenhearted" (Tehillim 34:19); "I dwell on high, in holiness; yet with the contrite and the lowly in spirit" (Yeshayah 58:15).*

Therefore the statement "The headings of chapters [of The Works of the Divine Chariot] may be transmitted to one student" is further narrowed down in the Talmud, as follows, "The headings of chapters may be transmitted only to the head of a Beis Din, and only if his heart is anxious within him" (Chagigah 13a), i.e. in whom wisdom is united with humility, meekness and fear of sin.

Now, consider how the Rabbis stipulated in their writings that before a person could be admitted to lectures on the mystical and metaphysical aspects of Torah, he had to be perfect in ethical conduct, in philosophy, he had to be astute, perceptive, eloquent, and able to convey ideas by hinting at them. In this connection the Gemara relates: R. Yochanan said to Rabbi Elazar: "Come, I will teach you The Works of the Divine Chariot." Rabbi Elazar replied: "I am not old enough." In other words, I still feel in me the hotbloodedness and the impulsiveness of youth. This teaches you that in addition to the above mentioned good qualities, a certain age is also required. This being so, how could anyone lecture on these metaphysical topics to an audience of ordinary people, including women and children.

UNDIVIDED ATTENTION

The Fifth Reason: [Often a person cannot concentrate on the abstract subject of metaphysics] because he is concerned with taking care of his physical needs and providing for his wife and children. This is surely so if he chases after luxuries, regardless whether this is his innate tendency or he is following

the trend of the time. Even the perfect man, if he is preoc-
cupied with running after necessities or after frills and luxuries, will weaken or lose his desire for meditation. He will
study only when the mood strikes, with indifference, and
without attention. He will not reach that which he is capable
of, and will acquire superficial and blurred knowledge. For
these [five] reasons it is proper that the subject of metaphysics be studied only by outstanding individuals and not
taught to the general public. It is not for the beginner, he
should stay away from it just as a little child has to be kept
away from indigestible food and from carrying heavy
weights.

CHAPTER 35

THE PUBLIC MUST BE TAUGHT
THE FUNDAMENTALS OF FAITH

In the preceding chapters we have discussed the importance of metaphysics, its esoteric nature, the complexity of
the subject and the need to withhold its knowledge from the
public. Don't think, that this means [that we should keep
from the public] the principle of the incorporeality Hashem
and the teaching that He is unaffected by any cause outside
Himself. This is not the case. For just as all people must be
informed, and children taught that Hashem is One, and that
no other god may be worshipped, so too all must be taught
that we have by tradition [from our ancestors] that Hashem
does not have a body, there is absolutely no similarity at all

between Him and His creatures, that His existence is not like the existence of His creatures; His life is not like that of any living being, His wisdom is not like the wisdom of the wisest of men, and that the difference between Him and His creatures is not merely in number [that He is One, and they are many], but that He is a different kind of existence. To put it another way: Everyone should be made to understand that our wisdom and His, or our power and His, do not differ quantitatively or qualitatively, for if you compare two things, [say, a horse and a sheep], one of which is strong and the other weak, they belong to the same class [they are both mammals], and can be included under the same definition [they are both animals]. The same is the case with all other comparisons; you can only compare things that belong to the same group, as has been explained in books on biology. [By contrast,] whatever applies to Hashem is totally different from our human characteristics; there is no common denominator between Him and ourselves. Therefore, His existence and that of any other being are totally different. Only the term "existence" is applied commonly, as I will explain.

It is enough if we teach children and ordinary folk that they should believe there is a Being Who exists, Who is perfect, Who does not have a body, Who is not a force inside a body, that this Being is God, Who is above all imperfection, and not subject to external influence.

But there are subjects [that should not be taught to the general public]. These subjects include questions about the attributes of Hashem and their meanings, about Creation, how the material universe emerged from His non-physical existence. Questions about His supervision of the world, His will, His perception, His knowledge of everything; questions regarding prophecy and its various levels, and how His names signify His Oneness, although He is called by more than one name. All these are very profound issues, the true, *secrets of the Torah,* the mysteries that are mentioned so often in the books of the Prophets and in the words of our Sages. They are subjects of which we should only mention the headings of the chapters, as we have already stated, and only in the presence of a person who has the qualities we mentioned earlier.

The principle that Hashem is incorporeal, that He cannot be compared to His creatures and that He is unaffected by outside influences, are things that must be explained to every man according to his intellectual level, and they must be taught as accepted tradition to children and women, to the foolish and the dimwitted, as they are taught that Hashem is One, that He preceded all things created, and that He alone should be worshipped. Without incorporeality there is no unity, for matter is not one, but a combination of substance and form, which are two separate things. Also, substance (matter) is divisible. When people have accepted this teaching and it has become ingrained in their minds, they may ask questions about things they read in the books of the Prophets [where corporeality is attributed to Hashem]. We must explain to them that these terms are used in a figurative sense, as discussed in this book. They will then come to believe with perfect faith in the unity of Hashem and in the words of the Prophets.

Those who are not bright enough to understand the true interpretation of these passages, and to grasp that the same word may have more than one meaning, should be told that this passage is clearly understood by the rabbis, but that they should be satisfied to know that Hashem does not have a body and that He is not subject to change, that nothing resembles Him, that He cannot be classified into the same grouping with anything else, that the words of the Prophets are true, and that there is an explanation for all seeming contradictions. All this needs to be said to these people. It is not right to leave them with the belief that Hashem has a body, or corporeal attributes, any more than they should be left with the belief that God does not exist, that there are more Gods than one, or that any other being should be worshipped.

CHAPTER 36

AVOIDING THE ERROR OF CORPOREALITY

Speaking of the attributes of Hashem, I want to explain in what sense we can say something pleases Hashem, makes Him angry, or infuriates Him, or, with regard to certain persons, that Hashem was pleased with them, or was angry or furious with them. But that is not really the subject of the present chapter.

Here is what I want to say. When you go over the whole Torah and the books of the Prophets you will not find the expressions, *burning anger, fury,* or *jealousy* applied to Hashem except in reference to idolatry. None except idol worshippers are called, *enemy, adversary,* or *foe.* For example, *"If you worship other gods. . . God's anger will then be directed against you"* (Devarim 11:16,17); *"Do not cause God's anger to be unleashed against you"* (ibid. 6:15); *"angering Him with the work of your hands"* (ibid. 31:29); *"But He pays back His enemies to their face"* (Devarim 7:10); *"since this is something that Hashem your God hates"* (ibid. 16:22). There are countless examples like these; if you will look at all the examples you come across in the books of Tanach you will find what I said is correct.

The Erroneous Idea of Idolatry

The prophets made it a point [to call idolaters *enemy, adversary* or *foe*,] because it concerns false ideas about Hashem. If someone thinks that someone is standing while, in fact, he is sitting, he does not veer from the truth as much as a person who believes that fire is under air or that water is under earth,[21] or that the earth is flat, or other things like that [which are all untrue]. The latter does not stray from the truth as much as a person who believes that the sun consists of fire, or that the heavenly expanse is a hemisphere and the like; and this third person is not as far from the truth as the man who thinks that the angels eat and drink and things like that. The latter again, does not wander from the truth as much as one who believes that something other than Hashem should be worshipped. For stupidity and disbelief concerning a great thing, i.e. a thing that has a high position in the universe, has a greater impact than stupidity and disbelief concerning things that occupy a lower place. By *disbelief* I mean the belief that something is different from what it really is; by *stupidity* I mean the failure to know things that can be learned.

If a person does not know the relationship between a cone and a cylinder, or that the sun is a sphere, it is not as bad as not to know whether God exists, or whether the world exists without a God. If a person assumes that the cone is half of the cylinder, [which is incorrect, since a cone is only about one third of the cylinder,] or that the sun is a round disk, it is not as harmful as to believe that God is more than One. You surely know that idolaters when worshipping idols do

---

21. The ancients believed that the physical universe was composed of four elements: fire, air, water, earth, in descending order. Thus, if someone believed that fire is under air or that water is under earth he was mistaken on both counts, since fire is above air, and water is above earth.

not believe that there is no God beside [these idols]; and no idol worshipper ever supposed the image made of metal, stone or wood created heaven and earth, and guides them. Idolatry is based on the idea that the idol represents the mediator between man and God. This is expressed in the following verses, *"Who would not revere You, O King of the nations?"* *(Yirmiyah 10:7); "And everywhere incense is offered to My name, for My name is honored among the nations"* *(Malachi 1:11).* The words, *My name* allude to the Being that the nations call the First Cause.[22] We have already explained this in our larger work [*Mishneh Torah, Avodah Zarah 1:1*], and no scholar will dispute this.

The pagan priests, although they believe in the existence of the Creator, deny Him that which belongs to Him alone, in other words, they deny that only He should be served and exalted as it says, *"And you should serve Hashem your God"* *(Shemos 23:25).* Through the worship of Hashem the belief in His existence becomes firmly implanted in the people's mind. The pagans allow worship of other beings. This causes the people to give up their belief in the existence of God, because the people only acknowledge ceremonies without understanding their meaning or the true character of the being they are worshipping. Because of this they were punished with death, as it says, *"You shall not allow any people to remain alive"* *(Devarim 20:16).* The purpose of this command is to eradicate false ideology so that others should not be corrupted by it. As it says, *"So that they will not teach you"* *(ibid. 18).*

The idol worshippers are called *enemies, haters,* and *adversaries;* and it says that whoever worships idols arouses God's jealousy, anger and fury. [Now, if people incurred the death

---

22. The reference is to Aristotle's view of God. He calls God the first principle and final cause of all the universe.

penalty for placing a mediator between man and God,] imagine how severe the punishment will be for a person who denies the existence of God Himself, and believes Him to be something He is not, that is to say, he believes Him to consist of two beings, that He is corporeal, that He is affected by outside causes, or he attributes to Him any imperfection whatever. That makes him worse than a person who worships idols, believing that these idols, being mediators, can do good or evil.

Therefore, keep in mind, that by believing in corporeality or in anything related to corporeality, you make Hashem angry, and you become His enemy, His adversary and His foe to a greater degree than by worshipping idols. If you want to make excuses for those who believe in corporeality and say they were brought up with this idea, or they were ignorant or dim-witted, then you must make the same allowance for idol worshippers; their worship is due to ignorance or to their early upbringing. Maybe you will say that the literal interpretation of Biblical verses sparks doubt in people's minds, but you must realize that idolaters too, were brought to their belief by false fantasies and fictitious imaginings. There is no justification for people of limited intelligence if they do not accept [the doctrine of incorporeality] from true philosophers. I do not consider a person a heretic if he is unable to prove the incorporeality of Hashem, but I do consider a heretic anyone who does not believe it, especially when they see that Targum Onkelos and Targum Yonasan avoid [when referring to Hashem] expressions implying corporeality as much as possible. This is all I wanted to say in this chapter.

CHAPTER 37

———◆———

THE MEANING OF פנים—*FACE*

The word פנים—*face* is a term that has diverse meanings, most of which have a figurative character. In its plain sense it denotes the face of a living being, as in, *"Why have all faces turned pale?"* (Yirmiyah 30:6); *"Why are your faces so worried today?"* (Bereishis 40:7). Many other examples can be cited.

Face also can stand for *anger*, as in, *"She no longer had her face (anger)* (1 Shmuel 1:18). Therefore, the term is frequently used with reference to Hashem in the sense of anger and fury, as in, *"The face (anger) of Hashem is against evildoers* (Tehillim 34:17); *"My face (anger) will go away, and I will lead you"* (Shemos 33:14); *"I will direct My face (anger)* (Vayikra 20:3); there are many other examples.

Another meaning of *face* is *the existence and presence of a person*, as in, *"He died in the face (presence) of all his brothers"* (Bereishis 25:18); *"And in the face (presence) of all the people I will be glorified* (Vayikra 10:3); *"He will surely curse You in Your face (presence)"* (Iyov 1:11). The word *face* is used in the same sense in the verse, *"Hashem would speak to Moshe face to face"* (Shemos 33:11), meaning, Hashem communicated directly with the core of Moshe's consciousness, bypassing any intervening thinking processes. Likewise, *"Come, let us look one another in the face"* (2 Melachim 14:8); [meaning let us speak heart to heart] and also, *Hashem talked with you [B'nei Yisrael] face to face"* (Devarim 5:4). What this means is explained in another verse, *"You [B'nei Yisrael] heard the sound of words but saw no image; there was only voice"* (ibid. 4:12).

Hearing a voice without seeing an image is called *face to face*. In the same way, the passage, *"Hashem would speak to Moshe face to face"* parallels, *"[Moshe] would hear the Voice speaking to him" (Bamidbar 7:89)*. The perception of God's Voice without the intervention of an angel is described as a *face to face* encounter. The word *face* must be understood in this sense in, *"My face will not be seen" (Shemos 33:23)*, meaning, My true essence, can not be comprehended.

The word *face* is also used as an adverb of place, in the sense of *in front of* or *nearby*. In that sense it is often used in relation to Hashem, as, *"in the face (front) of Hashem" (Vayikra 1:3)* According to Onkelos it is used in this sense when Hashem informs Moshe the limit of human intellectual understanding *"You will see that which is behind me but My face will not be seen," (Shemos 33:23)* which he translates *"Those who stand in front of Me will not be seen,"* meaning *Those who stand in front of Me cannot be comprehended.* Onkelos takes this as a reference to [spiritual] beings whose relation to Hashem is so that they are constantly before Him or close to him, which means that they are continually under God's close supervision. Onkelos considers knowable things on a lower level than these [spiritual beings], because [they are material] things which are a combination of substance and form. This is what the Torah had in mind when it says, *You will see that which is behind Me,* meaning, [*"You will be able to comprehend those]* beings from which I turn away, and which I cast behind Me." Later on you will hear my explanation of what Moshe Rabbeinu asked for [when he said, *"Let me have a vision of Your Glory" (Shemos 33:18)*].

פנים is also used as an adverb of time, meaning, *before*. For example, *"In former times in Israel" (Ruth 4:7)*; *"Previously You laid the earth's foundation" (Tehillim 02:26)*.

Another meaning of face is *consideration*, or *respect* as in, *"Do not give special face (consideration) to the poor" (Vayikra*

19:15); "and a person receiving face (respect)" (Yeshayah 3:3); "Who does not show face (consideration)" (Devarim 10:17) The word *face* is used in the same sense in the verse [in the priestly blessing], *"May Hashem turn His face toward you, and grant you peace" (Bamidbar 6:26)* meaning, *May God direct His providence toward you and grant you peace.*

CHAPTER 38

THE MEANING OF אחור—*BACK*

The word אחור—*back* has various meanings. It is a noun, meaning *back*, as in *"Behind the back of the tabernacle" (Shemos 26:12); "The spear protruded from his back " (2 Shmuel 2:23).* It is also used in relation to time, denoting *after,* as in *"nor did any [king] like him arise behind (after) him" (2 Melachim23:25); "Behind (after) these events" (Bereishis 15:1).* In this sense the word occurs very often.

The term *behind* is also used to express *to follow something* or *to emulate someone's character traits,* as in, *"Behind (follow) Hashem your God' (Devarim 13:5); "They shall walk behind Hashem" (Hoshea 11:10),* meaning, *follow His will, walk in the way of His actions and emulate His actions.* In this sense the word is used in, *"And you will see My back"* (Shemos 33:23), which means, you will have a vision of what follows from My existence, what is similar to Me, and is the result of My will, meaning, all things created by Me, as I will explain further on.

CHAPTER 39

———◦◦◦———

THE MEANING OF לב—*HEART*

The word לב—*heart* is a noun with multiple meanings, referring to the organ that is the source of life to all living creatures that have a heart, as in *"I drove them into Avshalom's **heart**" (1 Shmuel 18:14).*

Since this organ is in the middle of the body, it has been figuratively applied to express *the central or inner part of anything, [the core]*, as in, *"reaching the **heart** of heaven" (Devarim 4:11); "in the **heart** of a fire" (Shemos 3:2).*

It also stands for *thought*, as in, *"Did not my **heart** go along?" (2 Melachim 5:26)*, i.e., I was thinking of you, when this event happened. This is also the meaning of, *"You will then not stray after your **heart**" (Bamidbar 15:39)*, i.e. after the urging of your thoughts; *"Whose **heart** [i.e. his thoughts] strays from God" (Devarim 29:17).*

The term *heart* also denotes *advice*, as in, *"All the rest of Israel was of one **heart** (mind) to make David king" (1 Divrei Hayamim 12:39); "but fools die for lack of **heart** (sense)" (Mishlei 10:21); "My **heart** [i.e. my counsel] will not turn away from this as long as I live" (Iyov 27:6).*

Heart also stands for *will*, as in, *"And I will give you shepherds after My own **heart** (will)" (Yirmiyah 3:15); "Are you as wholehearted with me as I am with you?" (2 Melachim 10:15)*, i.e. Do you want honesty as much as I do? In this sense the word has been figuratively applied to Hashem, as in, *"who will act in accordance with My **heart** (wishes)" (1 Shmuel 2:35); "My eyes and My **heart** (i.e. My providence and My will) shall forever be there" (1 Melachim 9:3).*

The word *heart* also symbolizes *understanding*, as in, *"A hollow man will gain **heart** (understanding)"* (Iyov 11:12); *"A wise man's **heart** tends toward the right hand"* (Koheles 10:2), meaning, his understanding is occupied with perfect thoughts [on metaphysics]. There are many examples of this. It is in this sense [of understanding] that the word *heart* has been figuratively applied to Hashem, and in a few exceptional cases it is used in the sense of *will*. In each verse it must be explained according to its context. In the following passages it denotes *understanding*: *"Ponder it in your **heart**"* (Devarim 4:39); *"They do not give **heart** (thought)"* (Yeshayah 44:19). The verse, *"Hashem did not give you a heart to understand"* (Devarim 29:3) expresses the same thought as, *"You have been shown so that you may understand"* (ibid. 4:35).

However, in the passage, *"Love Hashem your God with all your heart"* (ibid. 6:5), I explain *with all your heart* to mean, *with all the powers of your soul*, in other words, with all the powers of the body, for they all originate in the heart [which pumps life-giving blood into them]. The meaning of the entire verse is: *You should make the knowledge of God the goal of all your actions*, as we have explained in our Commentary on the Mishnah (*The Eight Chapters, Chapter 5*) and in our Mishneh Torah,(*Yesodei Hatorah 2:2*).

CHAPTER 40

———◆———

THE MEANING OF רוח—*WIND, SPIRIT*

The word רוח—*wind, spirit* is a noun with multiple meanings. Its primary meaning is *air,* one of the four primary elements, [which are earth, air, fire, and water]. as in, *"And the air of God floated"* (Bereishis 1:2).

It also stands for *wind,* as in, *"And the east wind was carrying the locusts"* (Shemos 10:13); *"west wind"* (ibid. 19). In this sense the word occurs frequently.

It also has the designation of *breath,* as in, *"a fleeting breath ,not returning"* (Tehillim 78:39); *"that has in it a breath of life"* (Bereishis 7:15).

It also refers to that which remains of a person after his death and is not subject to destruction, as in, *"And the **breath** (spirit) returns to God Who bestowed it"* (Koheles 12:7).

Another connotation of *breath, spirit* is the divine inspiration that is emanated to the prophets and by which they prophesy—as we will explain when we discuss prophecy, to the extent that it can be dealt with in a treatise like this. For example, *"I will cause some of the **spirit** that you posses to emanate, and I will grant it to them"* (Bamidbar 11:17); *"When the **spirit** descended on them"* (ibid. 25); *"The **spirit** of Hashem has spoken through me"* (2 Shmuel 23:2). The word is often used in this sense.

Furthermore, *spirit* has the meaning of *intention* and *will, desire,* as in, *"A fool expresses all his **spirit**"* (Mishlei 29:11), i.e. his intentions and desires; *"Egypt shall be drained of **spirit**, and I will confound its plans"* (Yeshayah 19:3), i.e., her intentions will be frustrated and her plans will be confused; *"Who* *has plumbed the **spirit** of Hashem, or who is familiar with His plan, that he may tell us?" (Yeshayah 40:13)*, meaning, Who knows the order established by His will, or fathoms the way He guides the existing world, that he may tell us? We will explain this in coming chapters on Divine guidance.

Whenever *spirit* is used with reference to Hashem it [usually] has the fifth connotation [that of Divine inspiration], but in a few cases it has the last meaning, namely, *will, intention*. The word should therefore be translated according to its context.

CHAPTER 41

—==(●)==—

THE MEANING OF נפש—*SOUL*

The word נפש—*soul* is a noun with various meanings. In the first place it stands for the life-giving force of all living creatures, as in, *"everything that has in it a living **soul**" (Bereishis 1:30)*. It signifies also blood, as in, *"You shall not eat the **soul** (blood) along with the meat" (Devarim 12:23)*. Another meaning of *soul* is *the power of speech*, which is the distinguishing feature of man, as in, *"As Hashem lives Who has made us this **soul**" (Yermiah 38:16)* [i.e. gives us the power of speech]. It denotes also the part of man that remains after death, as in, *"The **soul** of my lord will be bound up in the bundle of eternal life" (1 Shmuel 25:29)*. Lastly, it stands for *will, wish, desire*, as in *"To imprison his princes with his **soul** (at his whim)" (Tehillim 105:22)*; *"You will not give him over to the **soul** (desire) of his foes" (ibid. 41:3)*. It is my opinion that *soul* has this meaning in the following verses: *"If you have the soul (desire) to help me bury my dead" (Bereishis 23:8);* *"Even if Moshe and Shmuel were to stand before Me [to intercede], My soul (will) could not be [won over] toward this people" (Yirmiyah 15:1)*, meaning, I do not favor them, I do not want to save them. Whenever *soul* occurs in reference to Hashem it signifies *will*. We likewise interpret *soul* as *will* in the passage, *"His soul (will) to cause misery for Israel ended," (Shofetim 10:16)*. Yonasan ben Uziel did not translate this verse at all, because he understood *soul* in the sense of *life-giving force*, and thought these words ascribe corporeal qualities to Hashem. He therefore omitted them from his translation. However, if *soul* is interpreted here in the sense of *will*, the meaning of the passage becomes perfectly clear. For in the preceding verses we read that Hashem removed His protection from B'nei Yisrael, so that their enemies came close to destroying them. They then cried and prayed for help, but Hashem did not deliver them. When their misery mounted and their enemies oppressed them, they sincerely repented. It was then that Hashem took pity on them, and His will to continue their misery and trouble ended. Keep this [interpretation] in mind, for it is extraordinary.

CHAPTER 42

———◦◉◦———

THE MEANING OF חי—*LIFE* AND מות—*DEATH*

The term חי—*life* denotes a growing and feeling organism, as in, *"Every moving thing that lives" (Bereishis 9:3);*

it also suggests recovery from a severe illness, as in, *"when he lived(recovered) from his illness"* (*Yeshayah 38:9*); *"They remained in the camp until they became alive (recovered)"* (*Yehoshua 5:8*); *"an area of living (healthy) skin"* (*Vayikra 13:10*).

מות signifies *death* and *serious illness*, as in, *"His heart died within him, and he became like a stone"* (*1 Shmuel 25:37*), meaning, his sickness was serious. That's why it says regarding the woman of Tzorfas' son, *"His illness grew worse until he had no breath left in him"* (*1 Melachim 17:17*) [to indicate that he had died]. For the expression *he died* could have suggested that he was gravely ill, near death, like the first verse we quoted.

Some of the Andalusian[23] commentators say [he did not actually[24] die but] stopped breathing, and no breath could be detected. This sometimes happens to people who are comatose or victims of suffocation, where it cannot be diagnosed whether they are dead or alive, this condition can last for a day or two.

The term *living* is applied many times in the sense of *gaining wisdom*, as in, *[Wisdom and understanding] will give life to your soul"* (*Mishlei 3:22*); *"For he who finds me [i.e. the Torah] finds life "* (ibid. 8:35); *"They [the words of the Torah] are life for those who find them"* (ibid. 4:22). There are many examples of this. In keeping with this metaphor, true ideologies have been called *life,* and false ideologies, *death.* Thus, Hashem says, *"See! I have set before you [a free choice] between life and good [on one side], and death and evil [on the other]"*

---

23. Andalusia is a region in southern Spain, bordering on the Atlantic, the Strait of Gibraltar, and the Mediterranean.

24. In reference to the aforementioned verse *"he had no breath left in him"* the Rambam explains that it used this language to make it clear that he died. These commentators explained the verse to mean that he stopped breathing but did not actually die.

(*Devarim 30:15*), showing that *life* is identical with *good,* and *death* identical with *evil.* In the same sense I interpret the phrase where Hashem says, *"so that you may live" (ibid. 5:30)* according to the traditional interpretation of *you will have it good.* Since this metaphor has become widely used, our Sages have coined the saying, "The righteous even in death are called living, while the wicked even in life are called dead" (Berachos 18a). Make sure that you understand this.

CHAPTER 43

THE MEANING OF כנף—*WING*

The word כנף—*wing* has several meanings, most of which are figurative. Its primary definition is *wing of a flying creature,* as in, *"every bird [and] every winged animal" (Bereishis 7:14); "any winged creature that flies in the sky" (Devarim 4:17).*

Next the word was applied metaphorically to the wings[25] or corners of garments, as in, *"on the four wings (corners) of your garment" (ibid. 22:12).* It was also used to denote the ends of the inhabited parts of the earth, and the corners that are most distant from populated areas. For example, *"So that it seizes the wings (corners) of the earth" (Iyov 38:13); "From the wing (end) of the earth we hear singing" (Yeshayah 24:16).*

Ibn Yanach [in his *Sefer Hashorashim*—Book of Etymo-

---

25. A bird spreads out its wings and therefore anything that is spread out or extending can be referred to as a wing.

logical Roots] says *wing* is also used in the sense of *hidden*,[26] comparable to the Arabic *kanafat alshay-I have hidden something*. Consequently he translates *"And your Guide will no longer be winged" (Yeshayah 30:20)* as, *"then your Guide will no longer be hidden or concealed."* It is a fitting explanation, and I think *wing* has the same meaning in, *"He must not reveal the wing (privacy) of his father" (Devarim 23:1);* also in, *"Spread your wing (intimacy) over your handmaid" (Ruth 3:9).* I think in this sense the word *wing* is figuratively applied to God and to angels, for in my opinion, angels are not corporeal, as I will explain. Therefore, the passage, *"[Hashem, the God of Israel] under Whose wings you have sought refuge" (Ruth 2:12)* must be translated, *In Whose intimacy you have sought refuge.* Wherever the word *wing* occurs with reference to angels, it means concealment.

You surely have noticed the words of Yeshayah, [in which he described Seraphs], *"Each of them had six wings; with two [wings] he covers his face, and with two he covers his legs and with two he flies" (Yeshayah 6:2).* The meaning is this: The cause of the angel's existence is hidden and concealed, this is meant by the covering of the face. The things which the angel causes, which are symbolized by his feet (see Chapter 28) are also concealed; for the actions of spiritual beings are hidden, and their nature cannot be understood except after exhaustive study. [The two wings symbolize] the two reasons why these things are hidden from us: one reason is, because of them, [i.e. because of their lofty nature], the other is because of us; that is to say, our inadequate understanding, and the difficulty we have in grasping abstract thoughts. Concerning the phrase, *"and with two [wings] he flies,"* I will devote a separate chapter (Chapter 49) explaining why flight has been attributed to angels.

---

26. The wings of a bird cover and conceal the bird's body besides being used for flight.

CHAPTER 44

---◆◆◆---

THE MEANING OF עין—*EYE, SPRING*

The word עין has several meanings. It means *well, spring* and *fountain,* as in, *"by a spring in the desert" (Bereishis 16:7).* Furthermore, it signifies *eye,* as in *"an eye for an eye" (Shemos 21:24).* It also stands for *supervision,* as in, *"Take him and **put your eyes on** (supervise) him" (Yirmiyah 39:12).* In this figurative sense, eye should be understood when it is used in connection with Hashem. For example, *"My eye and My heart shall be there forever" (1 Melachim 9:3),* meaning, *"My Providence and My attention;" "The eyes [i.e. the Providence] of Hashem your God are on [the land] at all times" (Devarim 11:12); "The eyes of Hashem are ranging over the whole earth" (Zechariah 4:10),* meaning, His Providence reaches everything on earth, as we will explain in future chapters when we will deal with the subject of Providence. But when the word eye is associated with the verb *to see,* as in, *"[Hashem] Open Your eyes and see" (Yeshayah 37:17); "His eyes behold" (Tehillim 11:4),* the phrase denotes perception of the mind, not perception of the senses. For every perception of the senses reflects change, and Hashem is the cause of change never changing, as I will explain.

CHAPTER 45

———◦◉◦———

THE MEANING OF שמע—*TO HEAR*

The verb שמע—*to hear* has various meanings. It means *to hear*, and also *to obey*. An example of its meaning *to hear* is, *"You must not let it be heard through your mouth"* (Shemos 23:13). *"The news was heard in Pharaoh's house"* (Bereishis 45:16). There are many examples like this.

There are also numerous examples of *hearing* being used in the sense of *to obey*. *"They would not listen to (obey) Moshe"* (Shemos 6:9); *"If they will listen (serve obediently)"* (Iyov 36:11); *"Shall we then listen to you"* (Nechemiah 13:27); *"Any man who does not listen to (obey) your commands"* (Yehoshua 2:18).

Another connotation of *hear* is *to know, to understand*, as in, *"a nation whose language you do not hear (understand)"* (Devarim 28:49). Whenever *hearing* occurs in reference to Hashem, and the plain meaning of the passage indicates that it denotes *to hear*, it must be taken in the sense of perceiving. For example, *"Hashem heard it"* (Bamidbar 11:1); *"He has heard your complaints"* (Shemos 16:7). In all verses like this mental perception is meant. However, when, according to its plain meaning the passage seems to signify *to obey*, it implies that Hashem answered the prayer of the supplicant and fulfilled his wish, or did not answer and did not fulfill his wish. For example, *"I will surely hear his cry"* (Shemos 22:22); *"I will listen, for I am compassionate"* (ibid. 26); *"Incline your ear and hear"* (2 Melachim 19:16); *"Hashem would neither listen to you, nor pay attention to you"* (Devarim 1:45); *"Though you pray at length I will not listen"* (Yeshayah 1:15); *"For I will not listen to you" (Yirmiyah 7:16)*. There are many cases where *hearing* has this meaning.

In the coming chapters I will elaborate on the subject of these metaphors and similes, so that your thirst for knowledge will be quenched. I will explain in detail [why the prophets felt a need to use these figures of speech], so that all your doubts will be removed.

CHAPTER 46

━━━━◎━━━━

WHY THE PROPHETS ASCRIBED
PHYSICAL ATTRIBUTES TO HASHEM

We already mentioned [in Chapter 33] that there is a great difference between knowing something exists and understanding its true essence. We can become aware of the existence of a thing by observing (1) its accidents i.e. its accompanying features, (2) its actions, or (3) the impact it makes on remote objects.

[The Rambam explains what he means by (1) "observing its accidents i.e. accompanying features":] For example, if you want to describe the king of a country to one of his subjects who does not know him, there are many ways you can describe him and prove that he exists. You could say the king is a tall man with a fair complexion and grey hair. If you said this, you would be describing the king by his accompanying features.

[The Rambam now explains the meaning of (2) "observing its actions":] Or you might say the king is the person who is surrounded by a throng of people, some on horseback and others on foot. Soldiers with drawn swords are before him, over his head banners are waving, and trumpets are blown before him; or he is the person who lives in the palace in that country; or the person who ordered the building of that wall, or the construction of that bridge; or you may cite similar things he did or ways in which he affected others.

[The Rambam now explains, (3) "the impact he makes on remote objects":] [The king's] existence can be demonstrated in a still more roundabout way. For example, if someone asked whether this country has a king, you would reply, "Of course. No doubt about it." If he asked, "How can you prove it?" You would answer, "You see this money changer over there. He is a frail person of slight build, and on the table in front of him he keeps a pile of gold coins. Now before him stands this poor man, tall and strong, begging for a donation the weight of a grain of barley, the money changer turns him down and angrily chases him away. If the poor man would not have been afraid of the king, he would have killed the money changer without blinking an eye, or pushed him away and taken as much money as he could carry. So you see that this country has a king, and the proof of his existence is the orderly functioning of the legal system of the country, which is based on the respect of the king and the fear of punishment."

In all three examples nothing has been said about the king's personality and his true essence by virtue of which he is king. [Nevertheless through these observations we become aware of his existence.] The same can be said about information regarding the Creator given to the general public in the books of the Prophets and the Torah. There was a need to teach everyone that Hashem exists, and that He is perfect in every way. We must teach He exists, not only in the sense that the earth and the heavens exist, but that He intrinsically exists, has life, wisdom, power, and creates, and that He possesses all the other attributes we must believe in, as will be set forth further on.

Hashem's existence was made understandable to ordinary people by the use of allegories and similes. Hashem's existence is conveyed by speaking of Him in terms of physical bodies, because ordinary people consider only the physical body as something really in existence. They believe something connected to a body, but is itself not a body, has a lower degree of existence than a tangible body, because it needs the body in order to exist. Surely, they cannot begin to imagine something existing that has no body and is not a force inside a body; it is beyond their comprehension. In the same way, the idea that He is living is conveyed by a metaphor taken from motion [i.e. Hashem comes, goes, ascends, descends, gives . . .] because the common man cannot visualize life without motion; he thinks that something that cannot move from place to place is not alive, although motion is not a definition of life, but only an accompanying feature of it.

The most familiar of the senses are those of hearing and seeing. The only way we can imagine the mind of one person communicating with the mind of another is by means of speaking, in other words, by the sound formed into words by the lips, tongue and other organs of speech. Therefore, when we are told that Hashem has a knowledge of something, [the prophets] portray Him to us as seeing and hearing, meaning He perceives and knows those things that can be seen and heard. When we are told He conveyed ideas to prophets who transmit them to us, they describe Him to us as speaking, they mean that messages from Him reach the prophets; and that is the concept of prophecy, as will be fully explained later.

The Prophets describe Hashem as working, because we cannot think of any method of producing something except by mechanical actions. They say He has a soul, to express that He is living, because in the popular view only things that have a soul are alive; although the word *soul* has many different meanings, as we discussed [in Chapter 41].

Now, since we perform all these physical actions only by means of bodily organs, we attribute to Hashem in a figurative sense the organs of motion, namely, the feet and their soles; the organs of hearing, seeing and smelling, like ear, eye and nose; and the organs of speech, like mouth, tongue and voice; organs for the performance of work, like the hand, fingers, palm and arm. To sum it up, these parts of the body are figuratively ascribed to Hashem, Who is above all imperfection, to tell you that He performs certain acts. These acts are only figuratively ascribed to Him; you know His Oneness is perfect, and these acts [such as seeing and hearing] are not instruments He needs to acquire knowledge. We say, for example, He has eyes, ears, hands, a mouth, a tongue, to express that He sees, hears, acts, and speaks; but seeing and hearing are ascribed to Him simply to indicate that He perceives. Thus you find in the Hebrew, cases in which the perception of one sense is interchanged with that of another; for example, *"See the word of Hashem" (Yirmiyah 2:31)*, which means, *Hear the word of Hashem,* because the meaning of the phrase is, *Perceive what He says*; similarly the phrase, *"See the odor of my son" (Bereishis 27:27)* has the same meaning as *Smell the odor of my son,* since it relates to the perception of the smell.

The bodily organs attributed to Hashem in the books of the Prophets are either organs of motion, indicating life; sensory organs, indicating perception; organs of touch, indicating action; or organs of speech, indicating the Divine inspiration of the prophets, as will be explained.

The purpose of all these indications is to instill in our minds the idea that there exists a living Being, the Maker of everything, Who also has a knowledge of the things He has made. The sole purpose of this chapter is to explain how bodily parts are ascribed to Hashem, Who has no imperfection, namely, that they are mere reflections of the actions usually performed by these bodily parts. Since in our human view these actions are perfect [as will be explained in Chapter 47] we attribute them to Hashem, because we want to express that He is most perfect in every respect. We pointed this out above when we explained the Rabbinic dictum, *the Torah speaks in the ordinary language of men.*

Examples of motion being applied to Hashem are: *"My footstool"* (Yeshayah 66:1); *"The place for the soles of My feet"* (Yechezkel 43:7).

Examples of organs of touch applied to Hashem are: *"The hand of Hashem"* (Shemos 9:3); *"with the finger of Hashem"* (ibid. 31:18); *"the work of Your fingers"* (Tehillim 8:4); *"And You have laid Your hand on me"* (ibid. 139:5); *"the arm of Hashem"* (Yeshayah 53:1); *"Your right hand, O Hashem"* (Shemos 25:6).

In the following examples organs of speech are attributed to Hashem: *"For it was the mouth of Hashem Who has spoken"* (Yeshayah 1:20); *"And He would open His lips to you"* (Iyov 11:5); *"The voice of Hashem is powerful"* (Tehillim 29:4); *"and His tongue like devouring fire"* (Yeshayah 30:27).

Sensory organs are attributed to Hashem in the following verses: *"His eyes behold, His gaze searches mankind"* (Tehillim 11:4); *"The eyes of Hashem ranging over the whole earth"* (Zechariah 4:10); *"You have kindled a fire in My nostril"* (Yirmiyah 17:4).

Of the internal organs of the body [which are generally not regarded as perfect and are therefore not used to describe Hashem,] only the heart is figuratively applied to Hashem, because *heart* also denotes *intellect,* and is the source of all life. In phrases like, *"That is why My bowels yearn for him"* (Yirmiyah 31:20) and *"The sound of Your bowels"* (Yeshayah 63:15), the word *bowels* is used in the sense of *heart.* For the term *bowels* has a general and a specific meaning; in its specific meaning it signifies *intestines*, but when used in a general sense it can represent any internal organ, including *heart*.

The shoulder is never used metaphorically in reference to Hashem, because the shoulder is used to transport things, and because it comes into close contact with the thing it carries. All the more so the organs of digestion are never used as attributes of Hashem; everyone can plainly see that they are symbols of imperfection.

In fact, all organs, both the external and the internal, are needed for the various activities of life; some—for example all internal organs—are essential to keep a person alive, others, such as the reproductive organs, are needed for the preservation of the human race; others are means of improving the condition of man and make him work efficiently, like hands, feet and eyes. They all tend to make his motions, actions and perceptions flawless.

Animals need motion in order to approach things that are good for them and to move away from things that threaten them; they need the senses to tell what is harmful and what is beneficial. In addition, man, by nature, has to do all kinds of work to prepare his food, clothing and shelter. And there are also certain animals that work. I do not believe anyone will doubt when I say the Creator does not need anything to continue His existence, or to improve His condition. [Now, since we have established that the only purpose of organs and senses is to stay alive, and to improve one's condition, and Hashem does not need anything,] it follows that Hashem has no organs, or, for that matter, that He has no body, that He is not corporeal. His actions are accomplished by His Essence, not by any organ. He has, beside His Essence, nothing that could be the cause of His action, His knowledge, or His will. I do not intend to discuss this subject in this chapter.

Our Sages formulated a statement of principle in which

they rejected out of hand the literal meaning of the physical attributes of Hashem mentioned by the Prophets. This statement shows you that the Sages repudiated the belief in the corporeality of Hashem, and did not think any person could make a mistake about it. That's why they use in the Talmud and the Midrashim phrases like those found in the simple meaning of the prophecies. They knew there could not be any doubt about their figurative character, or any danger that anyone would misunderstand their meaning; and that all such expressions would be understood as metaphors, designed to convey the idea of Hashem's Existence.

The metaphor became widely accepted [by the Prophets] whereby Hashem is compared to a king who commands, warns, punishes and rewards his subjects, and whose servants and attendants proclaim his commands and carry them out. Thus the Sages chose that figure of speech, used it often, and applied to Hashem such terms as *speech, consent,* and *refusal* of a king, and other usual acts of kings. In all these cases they were sure no doubt or confusion would arise from it.

The statement of principle I mentioned above is found in *Bereishis Rabbah (Chap. 27)*. It says, *"Great was the power of the Prophets; for they compared that which was created to its Creator. For it says, 'Upon the semblance of a throne, there was the semblance of a human form' (Yechezkel 1:26)."* Thus the Sages stated plainly that all those images which the Prophets perceived in prophetic visions, are images created by Hashem. This is true, for every image they saw in their prophetic vision had been created. How marvelous is the Rabbis' expression, *How great was the power of the prophets!* The Sages implied that they themselves found it difficult to understand; for whenever the Sages found a saying difficult to explain or an act that seemed improper they used the phrase *"how great was the. . ."*. For example, [the Gemara relates that] a certain Rabbi performed the act of *chalitzah*[27] with a small shoe, [whereas the law requires a large shoe], he performed it alone, [whereas the law requires the presence of ten adult males], and at night, [whereas the law requires that it must be done during the day]. Thereupon, another Rabbi exclaimed, "How great [is his audacity] to act on the [minority] view of one individual!" (Yevamos 104a). Here too the Sages meant to say, "How amazing is it that the Prophets had the courage to use metaphors to describe the Essence of Hashem, using attributes of physical beings that He created." Reflect about that. Our Sages stated in unmistakable terms that they deny the belief in the corporeality of Hashem; and when the Prophets saw in their visions forms and images of physical beings, *they were comparing that which was created to its Creator,* to use the words of our Sages. However, if after these explanations, someone will quibble and find fault with the Sages, [and say they incorrectly portrayed Hashem in a physical way], because he does not know or understand their intentions, the Sages will not be hurt by it.

CHAPTER 47

TOUCH AND TASTE ARE NOT ATTRIBUTED TO HASHEM

We have already mentioned several times that the books of the prophets never ascribe to Hashem anything people generally think of as a defect, or anything people

---

27. If a man dies childless, his widow is not free to remarry unless a *chalitzah* ceremony is performed. At the *chalitzah* she takes off the shoe of her husband's brother right foot. (Devarim 25:5-10).

cannot associate in their minds with the Almighty. [The Prophets stay away from such words,] although such terms may not be different from other terms used as metaphors in relation to Hashem. You might say all things ascribed to Hashem are considered in some way to be perfection, or can be imagined to be perfect.

According to this principle we must explain why the senses of hearing, sight and smell are attributed to Hashem, but not those of taste and touch; [nowhere does it say, "Hashem touched" or "Hashem tasted"]. After all, He is exalted far above the use of any of the five senses; they are all imperfect instruments of perception, [so, if one of the senses is applied to Hashem, all five should be attributed to Him]. [The senses are deficient] even for those who have no other source of knowledge, because they are passive, receive impressions from the outside world, and are subject to breakdown, aches and pains as much as the other organs of the body. When we say Hashem sees, we mean He perceives things that can be seen; when we say Hashem hears, we mean He perceives things that can be heard. In the same way we might say, *He tastes and touches* which would mean, *He perceives things that man perceives by tasting or touching.* [Why then are taste and touch not ascribed to Hashem?] For when it comes to perception, all senses are identical; if we deny the existence of one of them in Hashem, we must do the same for all the five senses; and if we ascribe the existence of one of them to Hashem, we must ascribe to Him all of them. Nevertheless, [on the one hand] we do find in the Torah such phrases as, *"And Hashem saw" (Bereishis 6:5); "And Hashem heard" (Bamidbar 11:1); "And Hashem smelled" (Bereishis 8:21),* but we do not come across the expressions, *"And Hashem tasted," "And Hashem touched."*

I believe the reason for this discrepancy is that it is accepted that Hashem does not come into physical contact with a body in the way that one physical body comes into direct contact with another, since He is not even seen by the eye. These two senses, namely, taste and touch, only come into play when they have direct contact with the object. In contrast, by sight, hearing, and smell even distant objects can be perceived. Therefore, in the popular mind-set it was considered fitting to apply these senses[28] to Hashem metaphorically.

Besides, the purpose of ascribing these senses to Hashem was to tell us that He perceives our actions; and hearing and sight are sufficient to describe that He finds out what a person does or says. Also our Sages, wanted us to be careful of our actions and warns us, "Know what is above you—a watchful Eye and an attentive ear" (Avos 2:1).

You know, however, that in reality, the status of all the senses is the same, and just as touch and taste cannot be applied to Hashem, sight, hearing and smell cannot be ascribed to Him either, for they are all physical perceptions and impressions which are subject to change. The only difference is that the drawbacks of touch and taste are recognized immediately, while sight, hearing and smell are considered as perfection.

In the same way, the flaws of the imagination are seen at once, while the imperfections inherent in thinking and reasoning are less obvious. Imagination therefore, was never used as a metaphor in relation to Hashem, while thought and reason are figuratively attributed to Him, as in, *"The thoughts that He thought"* (*Yirmiyah 49:20*); *"And by His understanding He stretched out the skies"* (*ibid. 10:12*). And so, the mental perceptions [i.e.imagination and thinking] were treated

---

28. We cannot see Hashem, but if we say Hashem sees, it is not difficult for people to comprehend because the sense of sight is applicable even from a distance. Since taste and touch are senses that are not applicable from a distance—one cannot touch or taste something without physical contact—we do not ascribe these senses to Hashem.

the same way as the sensory perceptions [i.e. sight, hearing, touch]; some are figuratively applied to Hashem, and some are not. It all depends on the language of man; he ascribes to Hashem what he considers perfect and does not ascribe to Him what he considers a defect. The truth is, however, that no attribute that adds something to His Essence, can be ascribed to him, as will be proved.

CHAPTER 48

TARGUM'S DISTINCTION BETWEEN
שמע—*HEAR* AND ראה—*SEE*

Whenever in the Torah the verb *to hear* is applied to Hashem, Onkelos, the Convert, does not translate it literally, but paraphrases it to mean a spoken word reached Him, i.e., He perceived it, or He accepted or did not accept it, when that spoken word was uttered in supplication or prayer. The words *Hashem heard* are always interpreted by him, *It was heard before Hashem,* or *He accepted,* when they refer to supplication and prayer, as in, *"I will hear their cry"* *(Shemos 22:22)* which he paraphrases, *"I will surely accept their cry."* Onkelos follows this principle throughout his translation of the Torah, without exception. But when it comes to the verb, *to see,* his interpretations vary in a peculiar way, and I was unable to detect a pattern or method. In some instances he translates literally, *and Hashem saw,* while in others he paraphrases, *it was revealed before Hashem.* Because Onkelos uses the Aramaic phrase "וחזה Hashem" to translate "and Hashem saw" we see clearly that this Aramaic term has more than one meaning, and signifies mental perception as well as visual sight.[29] This being so, I am surprised that, in some cases he avoids the literal rendering ["Hashem saw"] and substitutes for it, "And it was revealed before Hashem."

WHERE ONKELOS DOES PARAPHRASE SEEING

However, when I examined the various versions of Targum Onkelos, which I either found myself or heard from others during my studies, I found whenever the term *to see* is connected with unfairness, injury or violence Onkelos paraphrases it, *It was revealed before Hashem*. There is no doubt that the word חזה in Aramaic denotes clear perception and awareness of the object that is being viewed. Therefore, when Onkelos found the verb *to see* connected with unfairness [which he did not want to link directly to Hashem], he did not translate it literally, but paraphrased *It was revealed before Hashem*.

I noticed in all instances in the Torah where seeing is attributed to Hashem he translated it literally, except in these cases that I mention *"Hashem saw my troubles"* (Bereishis 29:32) which he translated: *My troubles were revealed before Hashem; "I have seen all that Lavan does to you"* (ibid.31:12) he translates *All that Lavan does to you is revealed before Me;*— although this was said by an angel [and not by Hashem], Onkelos does not ascribe to him the kind of perception that implies complete comprehension of the object, because the object is unfairness; [Lavan's unjust treatment of Yaakov];

---

29. Although Onkelos always paraphrases *action* verbs applied to Hashem to mean He perceived, he did not do so with the verb *to see*. Obviously the Aramaic word חזה—which we translate as *to see*—also has as a primary definition *to perceive*. Therefore there was no need to paraphrase it.

*"The oppression of the children of Israel was known before God"
(Shemos 2:25); "The oppression of My children was surely known
to Me" (ibid. 3:7); "The pressure is known to Me" (ibid. 9);
"Their misery is known to Me" (ibid. 4:31); "This people is
known to Me" (ibid. 32:9)*, meaning, their rebellion is known
to Me. Compare also, *"And God saw the children of Israel"
(ibid. 2:25)* which means *"He saw their misery and their trouble." "And it was known to Hashem, and He was offended"
(Devarim 32:19); "It was known to Him that their power was
gone" (ibid. 36)*; in this case the object of Hashem's perception was the wrong done to the children of Israel, and the
growing power of the enemy.

In all these examples Onkelos steadfastly sticks to his principle [of paraphrasing *to see* when its object is unfairness],
which can be summed up in the words, *"You cannot look on
iniquity" (Chavakuk 1:13)*. That is why he translates the verb
to see, when it refers to oppression or rebellion, as *It is revealed
before Him*. This is a fine and suitable explanation, and I do
not doubt its correctness. It is weakened, however, by three
passages where, according to this rule, I expected to find the
verb *to see* paraphrased as *to be revealed before Him*, but I
found instead the literal translation *to see* in the various copies
of the Targum. These are the passages: *"And Hashem saw that
man's wickedness on earth was increasing" (Bereishis 6:5); "God
saw the world, and it was corrupt" (ibid. 6:12); "Hashem saw
that Leah was unloved" (ibid. 29:31)*. [In these three examples
Hashem perceived unfairness, yet the Targum translates *He
saw*, and not *it was revealed before Him*.] It seems to me that
in these passages an error has crept into the copies of the
Targum. We do not have the original manuscript of Onkelos,
so we cannot find an appropriate explanation.

On the other hand, there is the verse, *"God will see to a
lamb" (Bereishis 22:8)* which Onkelos paraphrases, "The
lamb is known to God," [although it does not refer to

unfairness or iniquity. Why? The answer is this:] He either wanted to indicate that God was not expected to seek and to bring the lamb,[30] or he considered it unseemly, to connect God's perception with a dumb animal.

The various copies of the Targum must be carefully studied on this point, and if you still find those passages the same as I quoted them, I cannot explain the reason for the inconsistencies.

CHAPTER 49

METAPHORS APPLIED TO ANGELS

The angels, [like Hashem Himself,] are nonphysical; they are rational beings without bodies, but they are created beings, and Hashem created them, as we will explain.

In Bereishis Rabbah, our Sages say, "It says, *'God stationed the keruvim at the east [of Eden,] along with the flame of the revolving sword"* (Bereishis 3:24). In this verse the angels are called *the flame of the revolving sword* in keeping with the phrase, *"[He makes] His servants fiery flames"* (Tehillim 104:4). The sword is described as *revolving* because angels change their identity; sometimes they appear as males, sometimes as females; sometimes as spirits and occasionally as angels."

By this comment, the Sages clearly state that angels are intangible beings that have no permanent bodily form outside

---

30. Had he translated in this situation that *Hashem will see*, it could be taken to mean *Hashem will seek*, which is not the intent of the verse.

of the mind [of the prophet who imagines them as having a bodily form]. They exist entirely in prophetic vision, and depend on the power of [the prophet's] imagination, as we will explain when we discuss the true meaning of prophecy.

When the Sages said that the angels appear *sometimes as females* they had in mind the vision of Zechariah, *"I saw two women come soaring with the wind in their wings" (Zechariah 5:9)*. You know how difficult it is to form an idea of anything immaterial and entirely without physicality, [that you cannot conceive it] except after a great deal of study. It is especially difficult for someone who cannot tell the difference between intellect and imagination, and who relies mostly on his imagination. Such a person believes things he imagines actually exist, or could possibly exist, but things he cannot imagine do not, and cannot exist. Such people—and most thinkers fall into that category—can never discover the true solution to any problem, or clear up any uncertainty. Because of this difficulty the books of the Prophets say things which, when taken literally, imply that angels are corporeal beings that move around, have human form, receive commands from Hashem and carry out whatever He wishes. The Prophets use such expressions to convey the idea that angels exist and are alive and perfect, in the same way as we explained with reference to Hashem.

WHY ANGELS HAVE WINGS

Now, if the Prophets would have been content to describe angels in human form, people would believe their true essence to be the same as Hashem, since in reference to the Creator expressions are also used that imply that He has a body, that he lives, moves and has a human form. So, in order to set the record straight that the existence of angels is lower than the existence of God, the Prophets introduced into their description of angels certain forms of animals. This was done to show that the existence of God is more perfect than angels, just as man is more perfect than an animal. All the same, no part of an animal was attributed to angels except wings[31]. You cannot fly without wings any more than walk without legs. Those two forms of motion can only be imagined in connection with these two members [i.e. wings and legs]. The motion of flying has been chosen to symbolize that angels possess life, because it is the most perfect and exalted movement in the animal kingdom. People consider flying absolute perfection, so much so that they themselves wish they could fly in order to escape from harm and to get quickly to faraway places. That's why the motion [of flying] has been attributed to angels.

But there is another reason [why angels are described as beings that fly]. A bird in flight passes swiftly, one moment you see it, a moment later it vanishes from sight; now it is near you, and before you know it, it is gone. These are precisely the features that apply to angels, as we will explain below. Since the motion of flight—this imaginary perfection—is characteristic of the animal world it has never been attributed to Hashem in any way, shape or form. Don't be misled by the passage, *"[God] mounted a cherub and flew"* *(Tehillim 18:11)*, because it is the cherub [not Hashem] that did the flying. The metaphor only suggests the rapid arrival of the prophecy referred to in the verse. It is similar to, *"Mounted on a swift cloud Hashem will come to Egypt"* *(Yeshayah 19:1)*, meaning, the punishment prophesied in this chapter will come down quickly on Egypt. Neither should

---

31. Although the primary purpose of attributing wings to angels was to indicate that they are not on the level of perfection of Hashem, and we give them attributes of the animal kingdom -namely wings - nevertheless only wings were attributed to them.

you be misled by expressions like, "the face of an ox," "the face of a lion," "the face of an eagle," "the sole of the foot of a calf," that occur in the prophecies of Yechezkel (1:7 and 10). All these are explained in a different way, as you will learn later, and besides, [Yechezkel] only refers to the *Chayos* [a less spiritual form of angels]. These concepts will be explained, (Part 3, Chapter 1) albeit in veiled terms.

The motion of flying, which is frequently mentioned in Tanach, cannot be visualized without wings. That is why wings were given to angels to symbolize their existence, not as a reflection of their true essence. You should also bear in mind that whenever something moves very quickly it is said to fly, since flying implies high speed, as in, *"swooping down like an eagle" (Devarim 28:49)*. The eagle flies and moves faster than any other bird, and that is why it is used in this simile. Furthermore, wings are what enables a bird to fly; that is why the number of wings of angels in the prophetic vision reflect the number of [enabling] causes that set an event in motion, but that is not the subject of this chapter.

GLOSSARY

ADAM HARISHON – Adam the first man
ADAR – The twelfth Hebrew month
AGGADIC DERASHOS – Homiletic discourses
AVRAHAM – Abraham
AVSHALOM – Absalom

B'NEI YISRAEL – Children of Israel
BAMIDBAR – The Book of Numbers
BEIS DIN – Jewish court
BEIS HAMIKDASH – Holy Temple
BEREISHIS – The Book of Genesis

CHAVAKUK – Habakuk

DEVARIM – The Book of Deuteronomy
DIVREI HAYAMIM – The Book of Chronicles

EICHA – The Book of Lamentations

GEMARA – Talmud

HASHEM – God
HASHGACHAH – Divine Providence
HOSHEA – The Book of Hosea

IYOV – Job

KOHELES – Ecclesiastes

LAVAN – Laban
LULAV – palm branch take on Sukkos

MELACHIM – The Book of Kings
MISHLEI – Proverbs
MISHNAH – compilation of the oral tradition; it also refers to one
    paragraph of this compilation

MITZVAH pl. MITZVOS – commandment
MOREH NEVUCHIM – Guide for the Perplexed
MOSHE RABBEINU – Moses our Teacher

NOACH Noah

ONKELOS – A convert who wrote an Aramaic translation of the Torah

SHEMOS – The Book of Exodus
SHIR HASHIRIM – Song of Songs
SHLOMOH – Solomon
SHMUEL – The Book of Samuel
SUKKAH – hut used on Sukkos
SUKKOS – Festival of Tabernacles

TANACH – Scriptures
TEHILLIM – Psalms

VAYIKRA – The Book of Leviticus

YAAKOV – Jacob
YECHEZKEL – Ezekiel
YEHOSHUA – Joshua
YESHAYAH – Isaiah
YIRMIYAH – Jeremiah
YISRAEL – Israel
YOEL – Joel